EASY FRENCH PHRASE BOOK

Over 1500 Common Phrases
For Everyday Use And Travel

Lingo Mastery

www.LingoMastery.com

ISBN: 978-1-951949-08-2

Free Book Reveals The 6 Step Blueprint That Took Students
From Language Learners To Fluent In 3 Months

- **6 Unbelievable Hacks** that will accelerate your learning curve
- **Mind Training:** why memorizing vocabulary is easy
- **One Hack To Rule Them All:** This <u>secret nugget</u> will blow you away...

Head over to **LingoMastery.com/hacks**
and claim your free book now!

CONTENTS

INTRODUCTION

If you have finally decided to visit France, one of the richest countries in history and culture, then you can't help but consider the words, phrases, and ways of saying things that you will use in certain situations, which you must know before leaving. This is all the more important since the average awareness of English in France is not that good, compared to other countries.

Thanks to this book, we will see how to deal with many situations that can be simple, complicated, funny, or even not funny at all — all those real situations that a tourist will experience when, for example, they are seeking activities to do, order a perfectly cooked *filet mignon* in a restaurant, or simply don't want to be bothered.

Think of the souvenirs to bring back to a relative. Do you want to negotiate on the price or ask for a discount? It is certainly here that you will need to find the way to express yourself correctly.

Most of the time, a translation with the vocabulary at your fingertips is the best solution, and therefore, why not take precautions and study a few phrases that could amaze your fellow travelers or your interlocutors?

Of course, there are some obstacles to overcome. Let's see, for example, what can create difficulties at a phonetic level in the French language.

Pronunciation of French vowels

There are six vowels in the French language: A, E, I, O, U, Y.

The vowel A

'A' is usually pronounced like the 'a' in the English word "flat," widening the corners of the mouth (denoted by 'aa' in the guide). However, it is sometimes pronounced like the 'a' in the English word "father," opening the mouth more vertically (denoted by 'ah' in the guide), specifically when it appears with a circumflex accent (â), a grave accent (à), or when it is the last voiced letter in a word (i.e. the consonant or consonants following it are silent). It can be pronounced 'ah' in a few other places with no rhyme or reason, but more often than not, the 'aa' pronunciation will prevail.

Avis (opinion), *aa-vee*
Madame (lady), *maa-daam*
Bâtir (to build), *bah-teer*
Déjà (already), *day-zhah*
Gras (fat), *grah*

The vowel E

'E' has a variety of pronunciations, depending on its accent or lack thereof.

a) Without any accent, it is pronounced with pursed lips like the 'oo' in the English word "look," denoted by 'uh' in the guide. When it has no accent and is found at the end of the word, it is always silent.

Revenir (to return), *ruh-vuh-neer*
Petite (small), *puh-teet*
Cabane (shack), *kaa-baan*

b) With an acute accent (é) – a flat 'ay' sound like the 'a' in the English word "maple" but with the tongue motionless so it does not lengthen into a 'y' sound at the end. This is denoted by 'ey' in the guide.

Été (summer / been), *ey-tey*
Déménager (to move house), *dey-mey-naa-zhey*
Café (coffee), *kaa-fey*

c) With a grave, circumflex, or diaresis mark (è, ê, ë) – like the 'e' in the English word "error," slightly flatter than the 'e' in the words "set" or "deck." This is denoted by 'eh' in the guide.

Père (father), *pehr*
Très (very), *treh*
Fête (celebration), *feht*
Rêve (dream), *rehv*
Noël (Christmas), *noh-ehl*

2

The vowel I

The 'I' is always pronounced 'ee,' like the English word "meet," even when it has a circumflex accent (î) or a diaresis mark (ï). This is denoted by 'ee' in the guide.

Finir (to finish), *fee-neer*
Prix (price), *pree*
Dîner (to eat dinner), *dee-ney*
Egoïste (selfish), *ey-goh-eest*

The vowel O

The 'O' is always pronounced like the 'oa' in the English word "boat" (even with a circumflex accent, 'ô') but with motionless lips, not pursing toward a 'w' sound at the end. This is denoted by 'oh' in the guide.

Mot (word), *moh*
Rose (pink), *rohz*
Hôpital (hospital), *oh-pee-taal*

The vowel U

The 'U' is pronounced with tightly pursed lips and sounds like the 'ew' in the English word "hew" but with motionless lips that do not purse toward a 'w' at the end. Here again, a circumflex accent or a diaeresis mark do not alter the pronunciation. It is denoted by 'u' in the guide

Lecture (reading), *lehk-tur*
Salut (hello), *saa-lu*
Musique (music), *mu-zeek*

The vowel Y

The 'Y' is prounounced the same as the 'I,' like the 'ee' in the English word "meet." This is denoted by 'ee' in the guide.

Anonyme (anonymous), *aa-noh-neem*
Hyperbole (hyperbole), *ee-pehr-bohl*
Système (system), *sees-tehm*

Pronunciation of French diphthongs

There are more diphthongs than vowels in the French language, and each has its own unique pronunciation.

The diphthongs AI and EI

'AI' is pronounced like the French è, like the 'e' in the English word "set." This is denoted by 'eh' in the guide.

> Faire (to do), *fehr*
> Frais (fresh, cold), *freh*
> Américaine (female American), *aa-may-ree-kehn*
> Neige (snow), *neh-zh*
> Peine (penalty), *pehn*
> Seize (sixteen), *sehz*

Note: when the 'I' has a diaeresis mark (ï), 'A' and 'I' should be pronounced separately, 'aa-ee.'

> Haïr (to hate), *aa-eer*
> Naïve (naïve), *naa-eev*

The diphthong AU and triphthong EAU

'AU' and 'EAU' are pronounced like the French 'O' but with motionless lips, not pursing toward a 'w' sound at the end, similar to the 'o' in the English word "rote." This is denoted by 'oh' in the guide.

> Automobile (car), *oh-toh-moh-beel*
> Faute (fault), *foht*
> Beau (handsome), *boh*
> Niveau (level), *nee-voh*
> Panneau (panel), *pah-noh*

The diphthongs EU and ŒU

'EU' and 'œu' are pronounced similarly to the unaccented 'E' but with the lips pursed even more, like the 'u' in the English word "hurdle." This is denoted by 'uh' in the guide.

> Peur (fear), *puhr*
> Heureux (happy), *uh-ruh*

Feu (fire), *fuh*
Cœur, *kuhr*
Œuf, *uhf*

Please note that when 'EU' is found alone, it is the past participle of the verb "avoir" (to have) and should be pronounced as 'u' and not 'uh.'

J'ai eu (I had), *zhey u*

The diphthong OI

'OI' is pronounced like the 'wa' in the English word "water." This is denoted by 'wah' in the guide.

Boire (to drink), *bwahr*
L'oiseau (the bird), *lwah-zoh*

The diphthong OU

'OU' is pronounced with the lips completely pursed into a circle and motionless, like the 'oo' in the English word "moor." This is denoted by 'oo' in the guide.

Bouger (to move), *boo-zhey*
Outre (furthermore), *ootr*

Pronunciation of the nasal vowels and some specific French sounds

There are some French sounds that do not have any equivalent in English.

The first category is called the "nasal vowels," as they are pronounced by passing air through the nose and mouth, as opposed to the oral vowels already discussed, which only require passing air through the mouth. They are a combination of one (or two) vowels and a consonant.

The second category is combinations of letters with the diphthong 'IL,' which is pronounced like the 'y' in the English word "yes" and can alter the letters preceding and following it.

Let's start with the nasal vowels. Please note, these are ONLY nasalized when the letter following the combination is a consonant that is different

5

from the combination's consonant or if the combination itself forms the final letters of the word. If the combination is followed by a vowel or its consonant is doubled, the combinations are not nasalized but rather pronounced separately and normally. An example of each is given for all combinations, one followed by a consonant (nasalized), one by a vowel (not nasalized), and one with a doubled consonant (not nasalized) to show the difference.

The nasal vowels AN, AM, EM, and EN [ãn]

These are all pronounced like a nasalized 'aun' in the English word "laundry." The 'EN' only falls into this category when not at the end of a word, otherwise it joins the following category (ĩn). These are denoted by 'ãn' in the guide.

Letters	Nasal (foll. by consonant or final)	Not nasal (followed by vowel)	Not nasal (double consonant)
AN	Grand, grãn	Vanille, vaa-nee-y	Anneau, aa-noh
AM	Ambre, ãn-mbr	Amour, aa-moor	Ammener, aa-muh-ney
EM	Membre, mãn-mbr	Demi, duh-mee	Emmener, ahm-ney
EN	Endurer, ãn-du-rey	Tenue, tuh-nu	Ennuyer, ah-nu-ee-ey

The nasal vowels IN, IM, AIN, AIM, and EIN [ĩn]

These are all pronounced like a nasalized 'an' in the English word "angle." The 'EN' falls into this category when found at the end of a word; otherwise it is part of the previous category (ãn). These are denoted by 'ĩn' in the guide.

Letters	Nasal (foll. by consonant or final)	Not nasal (followed by vowel)	Not nasal (double consonant)
IN	Intéressé, ĩn-tey-reh-sey	Minaret, mee-naa-reh	Innover, ee-noh-vey
IM	Importer, ĩn-pohr-tey	Rime, reem	Immeuble, ee-muh-bl
AIN	Pain, pĩn	Laine, lehn	n/a

AIM	Faim, _fĭn_	Aim<u>e</u>r, _ehm-ey_	n/a
EIN	Peinture, _pĭn-tur_	Pein<u>e</u>, _pehn_	n/a
final EN	Examen, _eg-zaa-mĭn_	n/a	n/a

The nasal vowels ON and OM [ōn]

This one is pronounced like a nasalized 'o' in the English word "orange."

Letters	Nasal (followed by consonant)	<u>Not</u> nasal (followed by vowel)	<u>Not</u> nasal (double consonant)
ON	Tron<u>c</u>, _trõn_	Rhôn<u>e</u>, _rohn_	Ton<u>ne</u>, _tohn_
OM	Om<u>b</u>re, _õn-mbr_ Accom<u>p</u>lir, _aa-kõn-mpleer_ Com<u>t</u>é, _kõn-teh_	Om<u>e</u>ttre, _oh-mehtr_	Hom<u>me</u>, _ohm_

The nasal vowel UN [ūn]

This nasal vowel has only one formulation, 'UN,' and is always pronounced the same way, like the French word for "one" (un.) This is denoted by 'ūn' in the guide.

Letters	Nasal (foll. by consonant or final)	<u>Not</u> nasal (followed by vowel)	<u>Not</u> nasal (double consonant)
UN	Lun<u>di</u>, _lūn-dee_ Auc<u>un</u>, _oh-kūn_	Lun<u>e</u>ttes, _lu-neht_	Sun<u>ni</u>te, _su-neet_

The French specific sounds:

The sound AIL/AILLE

Pronounced 'ah-ee,' like the English word "eye." Denoted by 'ah-ee' in the guide.

Travail (work), _traa-vah-ee_
Bataille (battle), _baa-tah-ee_

The sound AY/EIL/EILLE

Pronounced 'eh-ee,' like the 'ay' in the English word "pay." Denoted by 'eh-ee' in the guide.

> Paysage (landscape), *peh-ee-zaazh*
>
> Soleil (sun), *soh-leh-ee*
>
> Abeille (bee), *aa-beh-ee*

The sound ILLE

Pronounced like the 'ee' in the English word "seeing" with a slight 'y' sound after. Denoted by 'ee-y' in the guide.

> Bille (marble), *bee-y*
> Grille (grid), *gree-y*

The sound EUIL/EUILLE

Pronounced just like the French 'eu' but with a 'y' sound after, denoted by 'uh-y' in the guide.

> Ecureuil (squirrel), *ey-ku-ruh-y*
> Feuille (leaf), *fuh-y*

How to pronounce the French consonants

Now that we've covered the French vowels, it's time to look at how consonants behave. Most consonants are pronounced as in English; however, you have to be careful with a few of them.

They can be doubled, but it does not change the pronunciation most of the time.

The consonant B

Same as the English 'B' but silent when final:

> Beau (handsome), *boh*
> Plomb (lead), *plõn*

The consonant C

Pronunciation of the 'C' depends on the letter that follows it, with a few easy exceptions.

C followed by a back vowel (A, O, or U) or a consonant

Hard, pronounced like K unless given a cedilla (ç), in which case it becomes soft, like S:

Café (coffee), *kaa-fey*
Collier (necklace), *koh-lee-ey*
Curieux (curious), *ku-ree-uh*
Crayon (pencil), *kreh-yõn*
Façade, *faa-saad*
Façonner (to shape), *faa-soh-ney*
Reçu (received), *ruh-su*

C followed by a front vowel (E, I, or Y)

Always soft, pronounced like S:

Place, *plass*
Ici (here), ee-see
Cycle, *seekl*

Double C, 'CC'

The first 'c' is hard, like K, and the second one follows the rules above, hard before a back vowel and soft before a front one:

Accord (agreement), *aa-kohr*
Accent, *aak-sãn*

C followed by an H, 'CH'

Pronounced like the 'sh' in the English word "should," unless found in the combination CHR:

Chameau (camel), *shaa-moh*

Cher (dear), *sheh-r*
Architecture, *aar-shee-tehk-tur*
Christophe, *kree-stohf*
Chrome, *krohm*
Chromosome, *kroh-moh-zohm*

The consonant D

Same as the English 'D' but silent when final:

>Douter (to doubt), *doo-tey*
>Addition, *aa-dee-syõn*
>Grand (large), *grãn*
>Retard (delay), *ruh-tahr*

The consonant F

Same as the English 'F':

>Ferme (farm), *fehrm*
>Affiche (poster), *aa-feesh*

The consonant G

Like the 'C,' the 'G' is hard before consonants and back vowels (A, O, U), denoted by 'g' in the guide, and soft before front vowels (E, I, Y), denoted by 'zh' in the guide. The hard version sounds like the 'G' in the English word "grab," while the soft version sounds like the 'G' in "mirage." Also, like the 'C,' when doubled, the first 'G' is hard, and the second one follows the rule based on the letter after it. It is silent when final.

>Gâteau (cake), *gah-toh*
>Goûter (to taste), *goo-tey*
>Guider (to guide), *gee-dey*
>Gérant (manager), *zhey-rãn*
>Agir (to act), *aa-zheer*
>Gymnase (gym), *zheem-nahz*
>Gloire (glory), *glwah-r*
>Rang (rank), *rãn*
>Aggrandir (to enlarge), *aa-grãn-deer*
>Suggestion, *sug-zhehs-tyõn*

<u>Note:</u> The combination 'GN' is nearly always pronounced 'ny' instead of 'gn' (with some exceptions, like "agnostique").

>Agneau (lamb), *aa-nyoh*
>Ignorer (to ignore), *ee-nyoh-rey*

10

The consonant H

'H' is always silent, regardless of its location in the word.

> Habiter (to live), *aa-bee-tey*
> Souhaiter (to wish), *soo-eh-tey*

The consonant J

Pronounced like the soft 'G' in the English word "mirage," denoted by 'zh' in the guide.

> Jardin (garden), *zhaar-din*
> Ajouter (to add), *aa-zhoo-tey*

The consonant K

Quite rare, it is only found in words of foreign origin like "kiwi" and "kayak." It is pronounced the same as the English 'K.'

The consonant L

Same as the English 'L.'

> Lire (to read), *leer*
> Allumer (to light), *aa-lu-mey*

The consonant M

Same as the English 'M.'

> Mer (sea), *mehr*
> Flamme (flame), *flaam*

The consonant N

Same as the English 'N,' except when part of a nasalized combination (see above).

> Noir (black), *nwahr*
> Annoncer (to announce), *aa-nõn-sey*

The consonant P

Same as the English 'P' but silent when final. The combination PH is pronounced 'f,' just like in English.

Projet (project), *proh-zheh*
Apporter (to bring), *aa-pohr-tey*
Trop (too much), *troh*
Téléphone, *tey-ley–fohn*

The consonant Q

Pronounced the same as the English 'K.' Though nearly always followed by a 'U' like in English, the 'U' is <u>always</u> silent in French, <u>not</u> pronounced 'kw' as in English.

Quart (quarter), *kahr*
Chèque (check), *shehk*
Acquérir (to acquire), *aa-key-reer*

The consonant R

This is very different from the English 'R.' It is instead a uvular 'R,' which is the sound made by the vibration in the back of the throat when gargling water. It is denoted by 'r' in the guide but should not be mixed up with the English 'R' made with the tongue in the front of the mouth.

Rapide (fast), *raa-peed*
Arriver (to arrive), *aa-ree-vey*

The consonant S

Same as the English 'S,' except when located between two vowels, in which case it is pronounced the same as the English 'Z.' Also, it is always silent at the end of words, with a few very rare exceptions.

Scolaire (academic), *skoh-lehr*
Assurer (ensure), *aa-su-rey*
Maison (house), *mey-zõn*
Phase, *fahz*
Planètes (planets), *plaa-neht*

The consonant T

Same as the English 'T' but does not change when followed by an 'H' (the English 'th' sound does not exist in French.) It can, however, take on an 'S' sound in the TION combination.

Sortie (exit, outing), *sohr-tee*

12

Attirer (to attract), *aa-tee-rey*
Vert (green), *vehr*
Thérapie (therapy), *tey-raa-pee*
Nation, *naa-syõn*

The consonant V

Same as the English 'V.'

Souvenir (a memory), *soo-vuh-neer*

The consonant W

Same as the English 'V.' It is quite rare in French, mostly found in words of foreign origin.

Wagon, *vaa-gõn*

The consonant X

'X' has a wide variety of pronunciations. The general rule is 'ks' like in English before consonants and 'gz' before vowels or the letter 'H.' However, in some instances, it may be pronounced like the English 'S,' the English 'Z,' or even remain silent.

Texte (text), *tehks-t*
Exemple (example), *eg-zãnpl*
Exhibition, *eg-zee-bee-syõn*
Deux (two), *duh*
Deuxième (second), *duh-zyehm*
Six (six), *sees*

The consonant Z

Same as the English 'Z' but silent when final.

Douze (twelve), *dooz*
Chez (home), *shey*

The French liaisons

In French, when a word ending in a silent consonant is followed by a word starting with a vowel or an 'H,' the consonant often becomes voiced. This euphonic technique is called a liaison, and it is one of the aspects of French pronunciation that can make it tricky to determine where one word ends and the next begins. It will be identified with the underscore symbol "_" in this guide.

Vous avez (you all have), *voo_zaa-vey*
Un homme (a man), *un_nohm*

Important note on stress and intonation:

French is a syllable-timed language, so equal emphasis is given to each syllable. This is quite unlike many other languages, such as English, Spanish, or Italian, which are stress-timed languages, meaning they only give emphasis to one syllable in each word - the stressed syllable - and reduce the vowels in the rest of the syllables.

In our Spanish and Italian guides, you will find the stressed syllable in each word is capitalized to denote where to place the emphasis, but in French, all vowels must be pronounced fully, and each syllable must be pronounced with equal stress.

In the majority of cases, if a syllable in a word or sentence is emphasized for cadence and intonation purposes, it will be the final one, but as a general rule, one should simply pronounce each syllable with equal emphasis and give the sentence the same intonation you would use in English (e.g. final upward inflection when asking a question, etc.).

COLORS

Gold
Doré
Doh-rey

Red
Rouge
Roozh

Orange
Orange
Oh-rãnzh

Yellow
Jaune
Zhohn

Green
Vert
Vehr

Blue
Bleu
Bluh

Light blue
Bleu ciel
Bluh syehl

Violet
Violet
Vee-oh-leh

Pink
Rose
Rohz

Brown
Marron
Maa-ron

Purple
Mauve
Mohv

White
Blanc
Blãn

Black
Noir
Nwahr

Gray
Gris
Gree

Silver
Argenté
Aar-zhan-tey

What color is that sign?
De quelle couleur est ce panneau ?
Duh kehl koo-luhr eh suh paa-noh ?

Is the cartoon in color?
Le dessin animé est en couleur ?
Luh deh-sĩn aa-nee-mey eh_tãn koo-luhr ?

Is this television show in color?
Cette émission télé est en couleur ?
Seht eh-mee-syõn tey-ley eh_ tãn koo-luhr ?

This is a red pen.
Ceci est un stylo rouge.
Suh-see eh_tũn stee-loh roozh.

This piece of paper is blue.
Ce morceau de papier est bleu.
Suh mohr-soh duh paa-pee-ey eh bluh.

What color is that car?
De quelle couleur est cette voiture ?
Duh kehl koo-luhr eh seht vwah-tur ?

What color are your clothes?
De quelle couleur sont tes vêtements ?
Duh kehl koo-luhr son tey veht-mãn ?

Is this the right color?
Est-ce la bonne couleur ?
Ehs laa bohn koo-luhr ?

What color is the stop light?
De quelle couleur est le feu d'arrêt ?
Duh kehl koo-luhr eh luh fuh daa-rey ?

Does that color mean danger?
Est-ce que cette couleur signifie un danger ?
Ehs-kuh seht koo-luhr see-nyee-fee ũn dãn-zhey ?

That bird is red.
Cet oiseau est rouge.
Seh_twah-zoh eh roozh.

What color is that animal?
De quelle couleur est cet animal ?
Duh kehl koo-luhr eh seh_taa-nee-maal ?

The sky is blue.
Le ciel est bleu.
Luh syehl eh bluh.

The clouds are white.
Les nuages sont blancs.
Leh nu-aazh sõn blãn.

That paint is blue.
Cette peinture est bleue.
Seht pĩn-tur eh bluh.

Press the red button.
Appuyez sur le bouton rouge.
Aa-pwee-yey sur luh boo-tõn roozh.

Don't press the red button.
N'appuyez pas sur le bouton rouge.
Naa-pwee-yey pah sur luh boo-tõn roozh.

Black and White
Noir et Blanc
Nwahr ey blãn

Look at all the colors.
Regardez toutes les couleurs.
Ruh-gaar-dey toot ley koo-luhr.

Is that a color television?
Est-ce une télévision couleur ?
Ehs un tey-ley-vee-zee-yõn koo-luhr ?

What color do you see?
Quelle couleur voyez-vous ?
Kehl koo-luhr vwah-yey voo ?

Can I have the color blue?
Puis-je avoir la couleur bleue ?
Pweezh aa-vwar laa koo-luhr bluh ?

What colors do you have for these frames?
Quelles couleurs avez-vous pour ces cadres ?
Kehl koo-luhr aa-vey voo poor sey kahdr ?

Don't go until the color is green.
N'allez pas tant que ce n'est pas vert.
Naa-ley pah tãn kuh suh ney pah vehr.

Colored pencils
Crayons de couleur
Kreh-yõn duh koo-luhr.

Coloring pens
Stylos à colorier
Stee-loh aa koh-loh-ree-ey

The sharpie is black.
Le feutre est noir.
Luh fuh-tr eh nwahr.

I passed with flying colors.
Je suis passé avec brio.
Zhuh swee pah-sey aa-vehk bree-oh.

Do you have this in another color?
Avez-vous ceci dans une autre couleur ?
Aa-vey voo suh-see dãn_zun ohtr koo-luhr ?

Do you have this in a darker color?
Avez-vous ceci dans une couleur plus foncée ?
Aa-vey voo suh-see dãn_zun koo-luhr plu fõn-sey ?

Do you have this in a lighter color?
Avez-vous ceci dans une couleur plus claire ?
Aa-vey voo suh-see dãn_zun koo-luhr plu klehr ?

Can you paint my house blue?
Pouvez-vous peindre ma maison en bleu ?
Poo-vey voo pĩndr maa meh-zõn ãn bluh ?

Can you paint my car the same color?
Pouvez-vous peindre ma voiture de la même couleur ?
Poo-vey voo pĩndr maa vwah-tur duh laa mehm koo-luhr ?

The flag has three different colors.
Ce drapeau a trois couleurs différentes.
Suh draa-poh ah trwah koo-luhr dee-fey-rãnt.

Is the color on the flag red?
Est-ce que la couleur sur le drapeau est rouge ?
Ehs kuh laa koo-luhr sur luh draa-poh eh roozh ?

NUMBERS

Zero	**Nine**	**Eighteen**	**Twenty-seven**
Zéro	Neuf	Dix-huit	Vingt-sept
Zey-roh	*Nuhf*	*Dee_zweet*	*Vĩnt-seht*
One	**Ten**	**Nineteen**	**Twenty-eight**
Un	Dix	Dix-neuf	Vingt-huit
Ũn	*Dees*	*Dee_znuhf*	*Vĩnt-weet*
Two	**Eleven**	**Twenty**	**Twenty-nine**
Deux	Onze	Vingt	Vingt-neuf
Duh	*Õnz*	*Vĩn*	*Vĩnt-nuhf*
Three	**Twelve**	**Twenty-one**	**Thirty**
Trois	Douze	Vingt-et-un	Trente
Trwah	*Dooz*	*Vĩn_tey-ũn*	*Trãnt*
Four	**Thirteen**	**Twenty-two**	**Forty**
Quatre	Treize	Vingt-deux	Quarante
Kaatr	*Trehz*	*Vĩnt-duh*	*Kaa-rãnt*
Five	**Fourteen**	**Twenty-three**	**Fifty**
Cinq	Quatorze	Vingt-trois	Cinquante
Sĩnk	*Kaa-tohrz*	*Vĩnt-trwah*	*Sĩn-kãnt*
Six	**Fifteen**	**Twenty-four**	**Sixty**
Six	Quinze	Vingt-quatre	Soixante
Sees	*Kĩnz*	*Vĩnt-kaatr*	*Swah-sãnt*
Seven	**Sixteen**	**Twenty-five**	**Seventy**
Sept	Seize	Vingt-cinq	Soixante-dix
Seht	*Sehz*	*Vĩnt-sĩnk*	*Swah-sãnt-dees*
Eight	**Seventeen**	**Twenty-six**	**Eighty**
Huit	Dix-sept	Vingt-six	Quatre-vingts
Weet	*Dee-seht*	*Vĩnt-sees*	*Kaa-truh-vĩn*

Ninety	Two hundred	One thousand	One million
Quatre-vingt-dix	Deux cents	Mille	Un million
Kaa-truh-vĩn-dees	*Duh-sãn*	*Meel*	*Ŭn-mee-lee-yõn*

	Five hundred	One hundred	One billion
One hundred	Cinq cents	**thousand**	Un milliard
Cent	*Sĩn-sãn*	Cent mille	*Ŭn-mee-lee-*
Sãn		*Sãn-meel*	*yahr*

What does that add up to?
C'est quoi le total ?
Sey kwah luh toh-tahl ?

What number is on this paper?
C'est quoi le chiffre sur ce papier ?
Sey kwah luh sheefr sur suh paa-pyey ?

What number is on this sign?
C'est quoi le chiffre sur ce panneau ?
Sey kwah luh sheefr sur suh paa-noh ?

Are these two numbers equal?
Est-ce que ces deux chiffres sont égaux ?
Ehs kuh sey duh sheefr sõn_tey-goh ?

My social security number is one, two, three, four, five.
Mon numéro de sécurité sociale est un, deux, trois, quatre, cinq.
Mõn nu-mey-roh duh sey-ku-ree-tey soh-syaal eh_tun, duh, trwah, kaatr, sĩnk.

I'm going to bet five hundred euros.
Je vais parier cinq cents euros.
Zhuh veh paa-ree-eh sĩn sãn_zuh-roh.

Can you count to one hundred for me?
Pouvez-vous me compter jusqu'à cent ?
Poo-vey voo muh kõn-tey zhus-kaa sãn ?

I took fourteen steps.
J'ai fait quatorze pas.
Zhey feh kaa-tohrz pah.

21

I ran two kilometers.
J'ai couru deux kilomètres.
Zhey koo-ru duh kee-loh-mehtr.

The speed limit is 30 km/h.
La limite de vitesse est 30 km/h.
Laa lee-meet duh vee-tehs eh trãnt kee-loh-mehtr luhr.

What are the measurements?
Quelles sont les mesures ?
Kehl sõn ley muh-zur ?

Can you dial this number?
Pouvez-vous composer ce numéro ?
Poo-vey voo kõm-poh-zey suh nu-mey-roh ?

One dozen.
Une douzaine.
Un doo-zehn.

A half-dozen.
Une demi-douzaine.
Un duh-mee doo-zehn.

How many digits are in the number?
Combien y a-t-il de chiffres dans ce numéro ?
Kõm-byĩn yah-teel duh sheefr dãn suh nu-mey-roh ?

My phone number is nine, eight, five, six, two, one, eight, seven, eight, eight.
Mon numéro de téléphone est le neuf, huit, cinq, six, deux, un, huit, sept, huit, huit.
Mon nu-mey-roh duh tey-ley-fon eh luh nuhf, weet, sĩnk, sees, duh, ũn, weet, seht, weet, weet.

The hotel's phone number is one, eight hundred, three, two, three, five, seven, five, five.
Le numéro de téléphone de l'hôtel est le un, huit cents, trois, deux, trois, cinq, sept, cinq, cinq.
Luh nu-mey-roh duh tey-ley-fon duh loh-tehl eh luh ũn, wee-sãn, trwah, duh, trwah, sĩnk, seht, sĩnk, sĩnk.

The taxi number is six, eight, one, four, four, four, five, eight, one, nine.

Le numéro du taxi est le six, huit, un, quatre, quatre, quatre, cinq, huit, un, neuf.

Luh nu-mey-roh du taak-see eh luh sees, weet, ũn, kaatr, kaatr, kaatr, sĩnk, weet, ũn, nuhf.

Call my hotel at two, one, four, seven, one, two, nine, five, seven, six.

Appellez mon hôtel au deux, un, quatre, sept, un, deux, neuf, cinq, sept, six.

Aa-puh-ley mõn_noh-tehl oh duh, ũn, kaatr, seht, ũn, duh, nuhf, sĩnk, seht, sees.

Call the embassy at nine, eight, nine, eight, four, three, two, one, seven, one.

Appellez l'ambassade au neuf, huit, neuf, huit, quatre, trois, deux, un, sept, un.

Aa-puh-ley lãm-baa-saad oh nuhf, weet, nuhf, weet, kaatr, trwa, duh, ũn, seht, ũn.

GREETINGS

Hi!
Salut !
Saa-lu !

How's it going?
Comment ça va ?
Koh-mãn saa vah ?

What's new?
Quoi de neuf ?
Kwah duh nuhf ?

What's going on?
Qu'est-ce qui se passe ?
Kehs-kee suh pahs ?

Home, sweet home.
La douceur du foyer.
Laa doo-suhr du fwah-yey.

Ladies and gentlemen, thank you for coming.
Mesdames et messieurs, merci d'être venus.
Meh-daam_zey meh-syuh, mehr-see dehtr vuh-nu.

How is everything?
Comment va tout ?
Koh-mãn vah too ?

Long time, no see.
Ça fait très longtemps depuis qu'on s'est vu.
Saa feh treh lõn-tãn duh-pwee kõn sey vu.

It's been a long time.
Ça fait très longtemps.
Saa feh treh lõn-tãn.

It's been a while!
Ça fait un moment !
Sah feh un moh-mãn !

How is life?
Comment va la vie ?
Koh-mãn vah laa vee ?

How is your day?
Comment se passe ta journée ?
Koh-mãn suh pahs taa zhoor-ney ?

Good morning.
Bonjour.
Bõn-zhoor.

It's been too long!
Ça fait trop longtemps !
Saa feh troh lõn-tãn !

Good afternoon.
Bonjour.
Bõn-zhoor.

How long has it been?
Ça fait combien de temps ?
Saa feh kõm-byĩn duh tãn ?

It's a pleasure to meet you.
C'est un plaisir de vous rencontrer.

Sey_tũn pley-zeer duh voo rãn-kõn-trey.

It's always a pleasure to see you.
C'est toujours agréable de vous voir.
Sey too-zhoor aa-grey-aabl duh voo vwahr.

Allow me to introduce Earl, my husband.
Permettez-moi de vous présenter mon mari, Earl.
Pehr-meh-tey mwah duh voo prey-zãn-tey mõn maa-ree uhrl.

Goodnight.
Bonne nuit.
Bon nwee.

May I introduce my brother and sister?
Puis-je vous présenter mon frère et ma sœur ?
Pweezh voo prey-zãn-tey mõn frehr ey maa suhr ?

Good evening.
Bonsoir.
Bõn-swahr.

What's happening?
Qu'est-ce qui se passe ?
Kehs-kee suh pahs ?

Happy holidays!
Bonnes vacances !
Bohn vaa-kãns !

Are you alright?
Ça va ?
Saa vah ?

Merry Christmas!
Joyeux Noël !
Zhwah-yuh noh-ehl !

Where have you been hiding?
Où est-ce que vous vous cachiez ?

Oo ehs-kuh voo voo kaa-shyey ?

Happy New Year!
Bonne année !
Bohn aa-ney !

How is your night?
Comment se passe votre soirée ?
Koh-mãn suh pahs vohtr swah-rey ?

What have you been up to all these years?
Qu'est-ce que vous faites depuis toutes ces années ?
Kehs-kuh voo feht duh-pwee toot sey_zaa-ney ?

When was the last time we saw each other?
C'est quand la dernière fois qu'on s'est vu ?
Sey kãn laa dehr-nyehr fwah kõn sey vu ?

It's been ages since I've seen you.
Ça fait une éternité depuis que je vous ai vu.
Saa feh un ey-tehr-nee-tey duh-pwee kuh zhuh voo_zey vu.

How have things been going since I saw you last?
Comment ça se passe depuis la dernière fois que je vous ai vu ?
Koh-mãn saa suh pass duh-pwee laa dehr-nyehr fwah kuh zhuh voo_zey vu ?

What have you been up to?
Qu'est-ce que vous faites ces temps-ci ?
Kehs-kuh voo feht sey tãn-see ?

How are you doing?
Comment allez-vous ?
Koh-mãn_taa-ley voo ?

Goodbye.
Au revoir.
Oh ruh-vwahr.

Are you okay?
Vous allez bien ?

Voo_zaa-ley byĩn ?

How's life been treating you?
Comment va la vie ?
Koh-mãn vah laa vee ?

I'm sorry.
Je suis désolé.
Zhuh swee dey-zoh-ley.

Excuse me.
Excusez-moi.
Ehk-sku-zey mwah.

See you later!
À plus tard !
Aa plu tahr !

What's your name?
Comment vous vous appellez ?
Koh-mãn voo voo_zaa-puh-ley ?

My name is Bill.
Je m'appelle Bill.
Zhuh maa-pehl beel.

Pleased to meet you.
Ravi de vous rencontrer.
Raa-vee duh voo rãn-kõn-trey.

How do you do?
Comment allez-vous ?
Koh-mãn_taa-ley voo ?

How are things?
Comment vont les choses ?
Koh-mãn võn ley shohz ?

You're welcome.
De rien.
Duh ree-yĩn.

It's good to see you.
Ça fait plaisir de vous voir.
Saa feh pley-zeer duh voo vwahr.

How have you been?
Qu'est-ce que vous faites ces temps-ci ?
Kehs-kuh voo feht sey tãn-see ?

Nice to meet you.
Enchanté.
Ãn-shãn-tey.

Fine, thanks. And you?
Bien, merci. Et vous ?
Byĩn, mehr-see. Ey voo ?

Good day to you.
Bonne journée à vous.
Bohn zhoor-ney aa voo.

Come in, the door is open.
Entrez, la porte est ouverte.
Ãn-trey, laa pohrt eh_too-vehrt.

My wife's name is Sheila.

Ma femme s'appelle Sheila.
Maa faam saa-pehl shee-lah.

I've been looking for you!
Je vous cherchais !
Zhuh voo shehr-sheh !

Allow me to introduce myself. My name is Earl.
Permettez-moi de me présenter. Je m'appelle Earl.
Pehr-meh-tey mwah duh muh prey-zãn-tey. Zhuh maa-pehl uhrl.

I hope you have enjoyed your weekend!
J'espère que vous avez passé un bon weekend !
Zhehs-pehr kuh voo_zaa-vey pah-sey ũn bõn week-ehnd !

It's great to hear from you.
Ça fait plaisir d'avoir de vos nouvelles.
Saa feh pleh-zeer daa-vwahr duh voh noo-vehl.

I hope you are having a great day.
J'espère que vous êtes en train de passer une belle journée.
Zhehs-pehr kuh voo_zeht ãn trĩn duh pah-sey un behl zhoor-ney.

29

Thank you for your help.
Merci pour votre aide.
Mehr-see poor vohtr ehd.

DATE AND TIME

January
Janvier
Zhãn-vyey

February
Février
Fey-vree-yey

March
Mars
Maars

April
Avril
Ah-vreel

May
Mai
Mey

June
Juin
Zhu-ũn

July
Juillet
Zhwee-eh

August
Août
Oot

September
Septembre
Sehp-tãmbr

October
Octobre
Ohk-tohbr

November
Novembre
Noh-vãmbr

December
Décembre
Dey-sãmbr

What month is it?
On est quel mois ?
Õn ey kehl mwah ?

At what time?
À quelle heure ?
Aa kehl uhr ?

Do you observe Daylight saving time?
Observez-vous l'heure d'été ?
Ohb-sehr-vey voo luhr dey-tey ?

The current month is January.
Nous sommes en janvier.
Noo sohm_zãn zhãn-vyey.

What day of the week is it?
On est quel jour de la semaine ?
Õn ey kehl zhoor duh laa suh-mehn ?

Is today Tuesday?
C'est mardi aujourd'hui ?
Sey maar-dee oh-zhoor-dwee ?

Today is Monday.
C'est lundi aujourd'hui.
Sey lũn-dee oh-zhoor-dwee.

Is this the month of January?
Ça c'est le mois de janvier ?
Sah sey luh mwah duh zhãn-vyey ?

It is five minutes past one.
Il est une heure cinq.
Eel eh un uhr sĩnk.

It is ten minutes past one.
Il est une heure dix.
Eel eh un uhr dees.

It is ten till one.

Il est une heure moins dix.
Eel eh un uhr mwĩn dees.

It is half past one.
Il est une heure et demie.
Eel eh un uhr ey duh-mee.

What time is it?
Quelle heure est-il ?
Kehl uhr eh_teel ?

When does the sun go down?
À quelle heure le soleil se couche ?
Aa kehl uhr luh soh-leh-y suh koosh ?

It's the third of November.
On est le trois Novembre.
Õn eh luh trwah noh-vãmbr.

When does it get dark?
À quelle heure il fait nuit ?
Aa kehl uhr eel feh nwee ?

What is today's date?
C'est quoi la date d'aujourd'hui ?
Sey kwah laa daat doh-zhoor-dwee ?

What time does the shoe store open?
Le magasin de chaussures s'ouvre à quelle heure ?
Luh maa-gaa-zĩn duh shoh-sur soovr aa kehl uhr ?

Is today a holiday?
Aujourd'hui c'est un jour férié ?
Oh-zhoor-dwee sey_tũn zhoor fey-ree-yey ?

When is the next holiday?
C'est quand le prochain jour férié ?
Sey kãn luh proh-shĩn zhoor fey-ree-yey ?

I will meet you at noon.
Je vous retrouve à midi.
Zhuh voo ruh-troov aa mee-dee.

I will meet you later tonight.
Je vous retrouve plus tard ce soir.
Zhuh voo ruh-troov plu tahr suh swahr.

My appointment is in ten minutes.
Mon rendez-vous est dans dix minutes.
Mõn rãn-dey-voo eh dãn dee mee-nut.

Can we meet in half an hour?
On peut se retrouver dans une demi-heure ?
Õn puh suh ruh-troo-vey dan_zun duh-mee uhr ?

I will see you in March.
Je vous verrais en mars.
Zhuh voo vey-reh ãn maars.

The meeting is scheduled for the twelfth.
La réunion est programmée pour le douze.
Laa rey-u-nyõn eh proh-graa-mey poor luh dooz.

Can we set up the meeting for noon tomorrow?
Pouvons-nous organiser la réunion pour demain midi ?
Poo-võn noo ohr-gaa-nee-zey laa rey-u-nyõn poor duh-mĩn mee-dee ?

What time will the cab arrive?
À quelle heure le taxi va arriver ?
Aa kehl uhr luh taak-see vah aa-ree-vey ?

Can you be here by midnight?
Vous pouvez être là à minuit ?
Voo poo-vey ehtr lah aa mee-nwee ?

The grand opening is scheduled for three o'clock.
La grande ouverture est programmée à trois heures.
Laa grand oo-vehr-tur eh proh-graa-mey aa trwah_zuhr.

When is your birthday?
C'est quand votre anniversaire ?
Seh kãn vohtr aa-nee-vehr-sehr ?

My birthday is on the second of June.
Mon anniversaire est le deux juin.
Mõn_naa-nee-vehr-sehr eh luh duh zhu-ŭn.

This place opens at ten a.m.
Cet endroit s'ouvre à dix heures du matin.
Seh_tãn-drwah soovr aa dee_zuhr du maa-tĩn.

From what time?
À partir de quelle heure ?
Aa paar-teer duh kehl uhr ?

Sorry, it is already too late at night.
Désolé, c'est déjà trop tard le soir.
Dey-zoh-ley, sey dey-zhah troh tahr luh swahr.

COMMON QUESTIONS

Do you speak English?
Parlez-vous l'anglais ?
Paar-ley voo lãn-gleh ?

What is your hobby?
Quel est votre passe-temps ?
Kehl eh vohtr pahs-tãn ?

What language do you speak?
Quelle langue parlez-vous ?
Kehl lãng paar-ley voo ?

Was it hard?
C'était dur ?
Sey-teh dur ?

Can you help me?
Pouvez-vous m'aider ?
Poo-vey voo mey-dey ?

Where can I find help?
Où puis-je trouver de l'aide ?
Oo pweezh troo-vey duh lehd ?

Where are we right now?
Où sommes-nous à l'instant ?
Oo sohm noo aa lĩn-stãn ?

Where were you last night?
Où étiez-vous hier soir ?
Oo ey-tyey voo ee-yehr swar ?

What type of a tree is that?
C'est quel genre d'arbre ça ?
Sey kehl zhãnr daarbr sah ?

Do you plan on coming back here again?
Vous comptez revenir ici ?
Voo kõn-tey ruh-vuh-neer ee-see ?

What kind of an animal is that?
C'est quel genre d'animal ça ?
Sey kehl zhãnr daa-nee-maal sah ?

Is that animal dangerous?
Est-ce que cet animal est dangereux ?
Ehs-kuh seht aa-nee-maal eh dãn-zhuh-ruh ?

Is it available?
C'est disponible ?
Sey dees-poh-neebl ?

Can we come see it?
On peut venir le voir ?
Õn puh vuh-neer luh vwahr ?

Where do you live?
Où habitez-vous ?
Oo aa-bee-tey voo ?

Earl, what city are you from?
Earl, vous venez de quelle ville ?
Uhrl, voo vuh-ney duh kehl veel ?

Is it a very large city?
Est-ce une très grande ville ?
Ehs un treh grãnd veel ?

Is there another available bathroom?
Y a-t-il une autre salle de bain disponible ?
Ee-yah teel un ohtr saal duh bĩn dees-poh-neebl ?

How was your trip?
Comment s'est passé votre voyage ?
Koh-mãn sey pah-sey vohtr vwah-yaazh ?

Is the bathroom free?
Est-ce que la salle de bain est libre ?
Ehs-kuh laa sahl duh bĩn eh leebr ?

How are you feeling?
Comment vous vous sentez ?
Koh-mãn voo voo sãn-tey ?

Do you have any recommendations?
Avez-vous des recommandations ?
Aa-vey voo dey ruh-koh-mãn-daa-syõn ?

When did you first come to China?
C'était quand votre première fois en Chine ?
Sey-tey kãn vohtr pruh-myehr fwah ãn sheen ?

Were you born here?
Vous êtes né ici ?
Voo_zeht ney ee-see ?

Come join me for the rest of the vacation.
Rejoignez-moi pour les restes des vacances.
Ruh-zhwah-nyey mwah poor ley rehst dey vaa-kãns.

What times do the shops open in this area?
À quelle heure les magasins s'ouvrent dans ce quartier ?
Aa kehl uhr ley maa-gaa-zĩn soovr dãn suh kaar-tyey ?

Is there tax-free shopping available?
Y-a-t-il des magasins hors taxes ?
Ee-yah teel dey maa-gaa-zĩn ohr taaks ?

Where can I change currency?
Où puis-je changer de l'argent ?
Oo pweezh shãn-zhey duh laar-zhãn ?

Is it legal to drink in this area?
Est-ce que c'est permis de boire dans cet endroit ?
Ehs-kuh sey pehr-mee duh bwahr dãn seh_tãn-drwah ?

Can I smoke in this area?
Est-ce que je peux fumer ici ?
Ehs-kuh zhuh puh fu-mey ee-see ?

What about this?
Et ça ?
Ey sah ?

Can I park here?
Je peux me garer ici ?
Zhuh puh muh gah-rey ee-see ?

Have you gotten used to living in Spain by now?
Vous êtes habitué à la vie en Espagne maintenant ?
Voo_zeht aa-bee-tu-ey aa laa vee ãn_nehs-paa-ny mĩn-tuh-nãn ?

How much does it cost to park here?
Combien ça coûte de se garer ici ?
Kõm-byĩn saa koot duh suh gah-rey ee-see ?

How long can I park here?
Pendant combien de temps je peux me garer ici ?
Pãn-dãn kõm-byĩn duh tãn zhuh puh muh gah-rey ee-see ?

Where can I get some directions?
Où puis-je obtenir des indications ?
Oo pweezh ohb-tuh-neer dey_zĩn-dee-kaa-syõn ?

Can you point me in the direction of the bridge?
Pouvez-vous m'orienter dans la direction du pont ?

Poo-vey voo moh-ree-ãn-tey dãn laa dee-rehk-syõn du põn ?

What can I do here for fun?
Qu'est-ce que je peux faire ici pour m'amuser ?
Kehs-kuh zhuh puh fehr ee-see poor maa-mu-zey ?

Is this a family-friendly place?
Est-ce un endroit plutôt familial ?
Ehs ũn_nãn-drwah plu-toh faa-mee-lee-aal ?

Are kids allowed here?
Les enfants sont autorisés ici ?
Ley_zãn-fãn sõn_toh-toh-ree-zey ee-see ?

Where can I find the park?
Où puis-je trouver le parc ?
Oo pweezh troo-vey luh paark ?

How do I get back to my hotel?
Comment je fais pour retourner à mon hôtel ?
Koh-mãn zhuh feh poor ruh-toor-ney aa mõn_noh-tehl ?

Where can I get some medicine?
Où puis-je acheter des médicaments ?
Oo pweezh aa-shuh-tey dey mey-dee-kaa-mãn ?

Is my passport safe here?
Est-ce que mon passeport est en sécurité ici ?
Ehs-kuh mõn paas-pohr eh_tãn sey-ku-ree-tey ee-see ?

Do you have a safe for my passport and belongings?
Avez-vous un coffre pour mon passeport et mes effets personnels ?
Aa-vey voo ũn kohfr poor mõn paas-pohr ey mey_zey-feh pehr-soh-nehl ?

Is it safe to be here past midnight?
Est-ce qu'il y a un risque de rester ici après minuit ?
Ehs-keel ee ah ũn reesk duh reh-stey ee-see aa-preh mee-nwee ?

When is the best time to visit this shop?
Quel est le meilleur moment pour visiter cette boutique ?
Kehl eh luh meh-yuhr moh-mãn poor vee-zee-tey seht boo-teek ?

What is the best hotel in the area?
Quel est le meilleur hôtel dans le coin ?
Kehl eh luh meh-yuhr oh-tehl dãn luh kwĩn ?

What attractions are close to my hotel?
Quelles sont les attractions proches de mon hôtel ?
Kehl sõn ley_zaa-traak-syõn prohsh duh mõn_noh-tehl ?

Do you have any advice for tourists?
Avez-vous des recommandations pour les touristes ?
Aa-vey voo dey ruh-koh-mãn-daa-syõn poor ley too-reest ?

Do you have a list of the top things to do in the area?
Avez-vous une liste des meilleures choses à faire dans le coin ?
Aa-vey voo un leest dey meh-yuhr shohz aa fehr dãn luh kwĩn ?

What do I need to pack to go there?
Qu'est-ce que je dois prendre pour y aller ?
Kehs-kuh zhuh dwah prãndr poor ee aa-ley ?

Can you recommend me some good food to eat?
Avez-vous des recommandations de bons plats à manger ?
Aa-vey voo dey ruh-koh-mãn-daa-syõn duh bõn plah aa mãn-zhey ?

What should I do with my time here?
Que dois-je faire de mon temps ici ?
Kuh-dwaazh fehr duh mõn tãn ee-see ?

What is the cheapest way to get from my hotel to the shop?
Quel est le moyen le moins cher pour se rendre de mon hôtel à la boutique ?
Kehl eh luh mwah-yĩn luh mwĩn shehr poor suh rãndr duh mõn_noh-tehl aa laa boo-teek ?

What do you think of my itinerary?
Que pensez-vous de mon itinéraire ?
Kuh pãn-sey voo duh mõn_nee-tee-ney-rehr ?

Does my phone work in this country?
Est-ce que mon téléphone marche dans ce pays ?
Ehs-kuh mõn tey-ley-fohn maarsh dãn suh pey-ee ?

What is the best route to get to my hotel?
Quel est le meilleur chemin pour se rendre à mon hôtel ?
Kehl eh luh meh-yuhr shuh-mĩn poor suh rãnd_raa mõn_noh-tehl ?

Will the weather be okay for outside activities?
Est-ce que le temps sera favorable aux activités en extérieur ?
Ehs-kuh luh tãn suh-rah faa-voh-raabl oh_zaak-tee-vee-tey ãn_nehks-tey-ree-uhr ?

41

Was that rude?
C'était impoli ça ?
Sey-tey ĩm-poh-lee sah ?

Where should I stay away from?
Quels sont les endroits à éviter ?
Kehl sõn ley_zãn-drwah aa ey-vee-tey ?

What is the best dive site in the area?
Quel est le meilleur site de plongée dans le coin ?
Kehl eh luh meh-yuhr seet duh plõn-zhey dãn luh kwĩn ?

What is the best beach in the area?
Quelle est la meilleure plage dans le coin ?
Kehl eh laa meh-yuhr plaazh dãn luh kwĩn ?

Do I need reservations?
Est-ce que j'ai besoin d'une réservation ?
Ehs-kuh zhey buh-zwĩn dun rey-zehr-vaa-syõn ?

I need directions to the best local food.
J'ai besoin de recommandations pour les meilleurs plats locaux.
Zhey buh-zwĩn duh ruh-koh-mãn-daa-syõn poor ley meh-yuhr plah loh-koh.

What's your name?
Quel est ton nom ?
Kehl eh tõn nõn ?

Where is the nearest place to eat?
Où est l'endroit le plus proche pour manger ?
Oo eh lãn-drwah luh plu prohsh poor mãn-zhey ?

Where is the nearest hotel?
Où se trouve l'hôtel le plus proche ?
Oo suh troov loh-tehl luh plu prohsh ?

Where is transportation?
Où se trouvent les transports ?
Oo suh troov ley trãn-spohr ?

How much is this?
Combien ça coûte ça ?
Kõm-byĩn saa koot sah ?

Do you pay tax here?
Est-ce que vous payez des taxes ici ?
Ehs-kuh voo pey-yey dey taaks ee-see ?

What types of payment are accepted?
Quels sont les modes de paiement acceptés ?
Kehl sõn ley moh-duh duh pey-mãn aak-sehp-tey ?

Can you help me read this?
Pouvez-vous m'aider à lire ceci ?
Poo-vey voo mey-dey aa leer suh-see ?

What languages do you speak?
Quelles langues parlez-vous ?
Kehl lãng paar-ley voo ?

Is it difficult to speak English?
Est-ce difficile de parler l'anglais ?
Ehs dee-fee-seel duh paar-ley lãn-gleh ?

What does that mean?
Qu'est-ce que ça veut dire ?
Kehs-kuh saa vuh deer ?

What is your name?
Quel est ton nom ?
Kehl eh tõn nõn ?

Do you have a lighter?
Avez-vous un briquet ?
Aa-vey voo un bree-keh ?

Do you have a match?
Avez-vous une allumette ?
Aa-vey voo un_naa-lu-meht ?

Is this a souvenir from your country?
Est-ce un souvenir de votre pays ?
Ehs ũn soo-vuh-neer duh vohtr peh-yee ?

What is this?
Qu'est-ce que c'est ça ?
Kehs-kuh sey sah ?

Can I ask you a question?
Puis-je vous poser une question ?
Pweezh voo poh-zey un kehs-tyõn ?

Where is the safest place to store my travel information?
Quel est l'endroit le plus sûr pour ranger mes documents de voyage ?
Kehl eh lãn-drwah luh plu sur poor rãn-zhey mey doh-ku-mãn duh vwah-yaazh ?

Will you come along with me?
Voulez-vous venir avec moi ?
Voo-ley voo vuh-neer aa-vehk mwah ?

Is this your first time here?
Est-ce votre première fois ici ?
Ehs voh-truh pruh-myehr fwah ee-see ?

What is your opinion on the matter?
Quelle est votre avis sur le sujet ?
Kehl eh vohtr aa-vee sur luh su-zheh ?

Will this spoil if I leave it out too long?
Est-ce que ceci va se gâter si je le laisse trop longtemps en plein air ?
Ehs-kuh suh-see vah suh gaa-tey see zhuh luh lehs troh lõn-tãn ãn pleh_nehr ?

What side of the sidewalk do I walk on?
Sur quel côté du trottoir je devrais marcher ?
Sur kehl koh-tey du troh-twahr zhuh duh-vreh maar-shey ?

What do those lights mean?
Que signifient ces lumières ?
Kuh see-nyee-fee sey lu-myehr ?

Can I walk up these stairs?
Est-ce que je peux prendre ces escaliers ?
Ehs-kuh zhuh puh prãndr sey_zehs-kaa-lyey ?

Is that illegal here?
Est-ce interdit ici ?
Ehs ĩn-tehr-dee ee-see ?

How much trouble would I get in if I did that?
Qu'est-ce que j'encourrais si je ferais ça ?
Kehs-kuh zhãn-koor-ey see zhuh fuh-reh sah ?

Why don't we all go together?
Pourquoi ne pas y aller tous ensemble ?
Poor-kwah nuh pah_zee aa-ley too_sãn-sãmbl ?

May I throw away waste here?
Puis-je jeter des déchets ici ?
Pwee-zhuh zhuh-tey dey dey-sheh ee-see ?

Where is the recycle bin?
Où est le bac de recyclage ?
Oo eh luh bak duh reh-see-klaazh ?

WHEN SOMEONE IS BEING RUDE

Please, close your mouth while chewing that.
S'il vous plaît, ne mâchez pas cela avec la bouche ouverte.
Seel voo pleh, nuh mah-shey pah suh-lah aa-vehk laa boosh oo-vehrt.

Don't ask me again, please.
Ne me redemandez pas, s'il vous plaît.
Nuh muh ruh-duh-mãn-dey pah, seel voo pleh.

I'm not paying for that.
Je refuse de payer pour cela.
Zhuh ruh-fuz duh pey-ey poor suh-lah.

Leave me alone or I am calling the authorities.
Laissez-moi tranquille ou j'appellerai la police.
Ley-sey mwah trãn-keel oo zhaa-peh-luh-reh laa poh-lees.

Hurry up!
Dépêchez-vous !
Dey-peh-shey voo !

Stop bothering me!
Arrêtez de m'embêter !
Aa-reh-tey duh mãn-bey-tey !

Don't bother me, please!
Ne me dérangez pas, s'il vous plaît !
Nuh muh dey-rãn-zhey pah, seel voo pleh !

Are you content?
Vous êtes content ?
Voo_zeht kõn-tãn ?

I'm walking away, please don't follow me.
Je m'en vais, s'il vous plaît ne me suivez pas.
Zhuh mãn veh, seel voo pleh nuh muh swee-vey pah.

You stole my shoes and I would like them back.
Vous m'avez volé mes chaussures et j'aimerais que vous me les rendiez.
Voo maa-vey voh-ley mey shoh-sur ey zheh-muh-reh kuh voo muh ley rãn-dyey.

You have the wrong person.
Vous vous trompez de personne.
Voo voo trõm-pey duh pehr-sohn.

I think you are incorrect.
Je crois que vous vous trompez.
Zhuh krwah kuh voo voo trõm-pey.

Stop waking me up!
Arrêtez de me réveiller !
Aa-reh-tey duh muh rey-veh-yey !

You're talking too much.
Vous parlez trop.
Voo paar-ley troh.

That hurts!
Ça fait mal !
Saa feh maal !

I need you to apologize.
Vous devez vous excuser.
Voo duh-vey voo_zehk-sku-zey.

Stay away from my children!
Gardez votre distance de mes enfants !
Gaar-dey vohtr dees-tãns duh mey_zãn-fãn !

Don't touch me.
Ne me touchez pas.
Nuh muh too-shey pah.

I would appreciate it if you didn't take my seat.
J'apprécierais que vous ne preniez pas ma place.
Zhaa-prey-see-reh kuh voo nuh pruh-nyey pah maa plaas.

You didn't tell me that.
Vous ne m'avez pas dit ça.
Voo nuh maa-vey pah dee sah.

You are price gouging me.
Vous me gonflez les prix.
Voo muh gõn-fley ley pree.

Please be quiet, I am trying to listen.
S'il vous plaît faites pas de bruit, j'essaie d'écouter.
Seel voo pleh feht pah duh bru-ee, zheh-say dey-koo-tey.

Don't interrupt me while I am talking.
Ne me coupez pas la parole.
Nuh muh koo-pey pah laa paa-rohl.

Don't sit on my car and stay away from it.
Ne vous asseyez pas sur ma voiture et gardez-en votre distance.
Nuh voo_zaa-sey-ey pah sur maa vwah-tur ey gaar-dey_zãn vohtr dees-tãns.

Get out of my car.
Sortez de ma voiture.
Sohr-tey duh maa vwah-tur.

Get away from me and leave me alone!
Dégagez et laissez-moi tranquille !
Dey-gaa-zhey ey leh-sey mwah trãn-keel !

You're being rude.
Vous êtes grossier.
Voo_zeht groh-syey.

Please don't curse around my children.
S'il vous plait ne jurez pas devant mes enfants.
Seel voo pleh nuh zhu-rey pah duh-vãn mey_zãn-fãn.

Let go of me!
Lâchez-moi !
Lah-shey mwah !

I'm not going to tell you again.
Je vais pas vous le redire.
Zhuh veh pah voo luh ruh-deer.

Don't yell at me.
Ne me gueuler pas dessus.
Nuh muh guh-ley pah duh-su.

Please lower your voice.
S'il vous plaît baissez votre voix.
Seel voo pleh beh-sey vohtr vwah.

What is the problem?
Quel est le problème ?
Kehl eh luh proh-blehm ?

I would appreciate if you didn't take pictures of me.
Je ne veux pas que vous me preniez en photo.
Zhuh nuh vuh pah kuh voo muh pruh-nyey ãn foh-toh.

I am very disappointed in the way you are behaving.
Je suis très déçu de votre comportement.
Zhuh swee treh dey-su duh vohtr kõn-pohr-tuh-mãn.

Watch where you are walking!
Attention où vous marchez !
Aa-tãn-syõn oo voo maar-shey !

He just bumped into me!
Il vient de me heurté !
Eel vyĩn duh muh ur-tey !

MEDICAL

I would like to set up an appointment with my doctor.
J'aimerais prendre rendez-vous avec mon médecin.
Zheh-muh-reh prãndr rãn-dey-voo aa-vehk mõn meyd-sĩn.

I am a new patient and need to fill out forms.
Je suis un nouveau patient, et je dois remplir des formulaires.
Zhuh swee_zũn noo-voh paa-syãn ey zhuh dwah rãn-pleer dey fohr-mu-lehr.

I am allergic to certain medications.
Je suis allergique à certains médicaments.
Zhuh swee_zaa-lehr-zheek aa sehr-tĩn mey-dee-kaa-mãn.

That is where it hurts.
C'est là que ça fait mal.
Sey lah kuh saa feh maal.

I have had the flu for three weeks.
J'ai la grippe depuis trois semaines.
Zhey laa greep duh-pwee trwah smehn.

It hurts when I walk on that foot.
Ça fait mal quand je marche sur ce pied.
Saa feh maal kãn zhuh maarsh sur suh pyey.

When is my next appointment?
C'est pour quand mon prochain rendez-vous ?
Sey poor kãn mõn proh-shĩn rãn-dey-voo ?

Does my insurance cover this?
Est-ce couvert par mon assurance ?
Ehs koo-vehr paar mõn_naa-su-rãns ?

Do you want to take a look at my throat?
Voulez-vous examiner ma gorge ?
Voo-ley voo ehg-zaa-mee-ney maa gohrzh ?

Do I need to fast before going there?
Dois-je être à jeun avant d'y aller ?
Dwahzh ehtr aa zhũn aa-vãn dee aa-ley ?

Is there a generic version of this medicine?
Y a-t-il un générique pour ce médicament ?
Ee_yah teel un zhey-ney-reek poor suh mey-dee-kaa-mãn ?

I need to get back on dialysis.
Je dois me remettre en dialyse.
Zhuh dwah muh ruh-mehtr ãn dee-aa-leez.

My blood type is A.
Mon groupe sanguin est A.
Mõn groop sãn-gĩn eh ah.

I will be more than happy to donate blood.
Ça me ferait plaisir de faire un don de sang.

Saa muh fuh-reh pley-zeer duh fehr ũn dõn duh sãn.

I have been feeling dizzy.
J'ai des vertiges.
Zhey dey vehr-teezh.

The condition is getting worse.
La condition s'empire.
Laa kõn-dee-syõn sãn-peer.

The medicine has made the condition a little better, but it is still there.
Le médicament a amélioré un peu la condition, mais elle est toujours présente.
Luh mey-dee-kaa-mãn ah aa-mey-lee-oh-rey ũn puh laa kõn-dee-syõn, meh ehl eh too-zhoor prey-zãnt.

Is my initial health examination tomorrow?
C'est demain mon premier examen de santé ?
Sey duh-mĩn mon pruh-myey_regz-aa-mĩn duh sãn-tey ?

I would like to switch doctors.
J'aimerais changer de médecin.
Zheh-muh-reh shãn-zhey duh meyd-sĩn.

Can you check my blood pressure?
Pouvez-vous vérifier ma tension artérielle ?
Poo-vey voo vey-ree-fyey maa tãn-syõn aar-tey-ryehl ?

I have a fever that won't go away.
J'ai une fièvre persistante.
Zhey un fyeh-vruh pehr-see-stãnt.

I think my arm is broken.
Je pense que mon bras est cassé.
Zhuh pãns kuh mõn brah eh kah-sey.

I think I have a concussion.
Je pense que j'ai une commotion cérébrale.
Zhuh pãns kuh zhey un koh-moh-syõn sey-rey-braal.

My eyes refuse to focus.
Mes yeux ne veulent pas se focaliser.
Mey_zyuh nuh vuhl pah suh foh-kaa-lee-zey.

I have double vision.
Je vois double.
Zhuh vwah doobl.

Is surgery the only way to fix this?
La chirurgie est-elle le seul recours ?
Laa shee-rur-zhee ey_tehl luh suhl ruh-koor ?

Who are you referring me to?
À qui me référez-vous ?
Aa kee muh rey-fey-rey voo ?

Where is the waiting room?
Où se trouve la salle d'attente ?
Oo suh troov laa saal daa-tãnt ?

Can I bring someone with me into the office?
Puis-je amener quelqu'un avec moi dans le bureau ?
Pweezh ah-muh-ney kehl-kũn aa-vehk mwaa dãn luh bu-roh ?

I need help filling out these forms.
J'ai besoin d'aide pour remplir ces formulaires.
Zhey buh-zwĩn dehd poor rãm-pleer sey fohr-mu-lehr.

Do you take Cobra as an insurance provider?
Prenez-vous Cobra comme assurance ?
Pruh-ney voo koh-brah kohm aa-su-rãns ?

What is my copayment?
Quelle est ma quote-part ?
Kehl eh maa koht-pahr ?

What forms of payment do you accept?
Quels modes de paiement acceptez-vous ?
Kehl mohd duh pey-mãn aak-sehp-tey voo ?

Do you have a payment plan, or is it all due now?
Vous avez un plan de paiement, ou il faut tout régler maintenant ?
Voo_zaa-vey ũn plãn duh pey-mãn, oo eel foh too rey-gley mĩn-tuh-nãn ?

My old doctor prescribed something different.
Mon ancien médecin me préscrivait autre chose.
Mõn_nãn-syĩn mehd-sĩn muh prey-skree-veh oh-truh shohz.

Will you take a look at my leg?
Pouvez-vous regarder ma jambe ?
Poo-vey voo ruh-gaar-dey maa zhãmb ?

I need to be referred to a gynecologist.
J'ai besoin qu'on me réfère à un gynécologue.
Zhey buh-zwĩn kõn muh rey-fehr aa ũn zhee-ney-koh-log.

I am unhappy with the medicine you prescribed me.
Je ne suis pas satisfait du médicament que vous m'avez prescrit.
Zhuh nuh swee pah saa-tees-feh du mey-dee-kaa-mãn kuh voo maa-vey prey-skree.

Do you see patients on the weekend?
Consultez-vous le week-end ?
Kõn-sul-tey voo luh wee-kehnd ?

I need a good therapist.
J'ai besoin d'un bon thérapeute.
Zhey buh-zwĩn dũn bõn tey-raa-puht.

How long will it take me to rehab this injury?
Combien de temps il me faudra pour me remettre de cette blessure ?
Kõm-byĩn duh tãn eel muh foh-drah poor muh ruh-mehtr duh seht bleh-sur ?

I have not gone to the bathroom in over a week.
Je ne suis pas allé aux toilettes depuis plus d'une semaine.
Zhuh nuh swee pah_zaa-ley oh twah-leht duh-pwee plus dun suh-mehn.

I am constipated and feel bloated.
Je suis constipé, et je me sens ballonné.
Zhuh swee kõn-stee-pey ey zhuh muh sãn baa-loh-ney.

It hurts when I go to the bathroom.
Ça fait mal quand je vais aux toilettes.
Saa feh maal kãn zhuh veh oh twah-leht.

I have not slept well at all since getting here.
Je n'ai pas du tout bien dormi depuis mon arrivée.
Zhuh ney pah du too byĩn dohr-mee duh-pwee mõn_naa-ree-vey.

Do you have any pain killers?
Avez-vous des antidouleurs ?
Aa-vey voo dey_zãn-tee-doo-luhr ?

I am allergic to that medicine.
Je suis allergique à ce médicament.
Zhuh swee_zah-lehr-zheek aa suh mey-dee-kaa-mãn.

How long will I be under observation?
Combien de temps je dois rester sous observation ?
Kõm-byĩn duh tãn zhuh dwah rehs-tey soo_zohb-sehr-vaa-syõn ?

I have a toothache.
J'ai un mal de dents.
Zhey ũn maal duh dãn.

Do I need to see a dentist?
Est-ce que je dois voir un dentiste ?
Ehs-kuh zhuh dwah vwahr ũn dãn-teest ?

Does my insurance cover dental?
Est-ce que mon assurance prend en charge les soins dentaires ?
Ehs-kuh mõn_naa-su-rãns prãn ãn shaarzh ley swĩn dãn-tehr ?

My diarrhea won't go away.
J'ai des diarrhées persistantes.
Zhey dey dee-aa-rey pehr-see-stãnt.

Can I have a copy of the receipt for my insurance?
Puis-je avoir une copie du reçu pour mon assurance ?
Pweezh aa-vwahr un koh-pee du ruh-su poor mõn_naa-su-rãns ?

I need a pregnancy test.
J'ai besoin d'un test de grossesse.
Zhey buh-zwĩn dũn tehst duh groh-sehs.

I think I may be pregnant.
Je pense que je suis enceinte.
Zhuh pãns kuh zhuh swee_zãn-sĩnt.

Can we please see a pediatrician?
Pouvons-nous voir un pédiatre s'il vous plaît ?
Poo-võn noo vwahr ũn pey-dee-ahtr seel voo pleh ?

I have had troubles breathing.
J'ai eu du mal à respirer.
Zhey u du maal aa rehs-pee-rey.

My sinuses are acting up.
Mes sinus me dérangent.
Mey see-nus muh dey-rãnzh.

Will I still be able to breastfeed?
Pourrais-je encore allaiter ?
Poo-rehzh ãn-kahr aa-ley-tey ?

How long do I have to stay in bed?
Combien de temps je dois rester au lit ?
Kõm-byĩn duh tãn zhuh dwah rehs-tey oh lee ?

How long do I have to stay under hospital care?
Combien de temps je dois rester hospitalisé ?
Kõm-byĩn duh tãn zhuh dwah rehs-tey ohs-pee-taa-lee-zey ?

Is it contagious?
Est-ce contagieux ?
Ehs kõn-taa-zhyuh ?

How far along am I?
Je suis à combien de mois ?
Zhuh swee_zaa kõm-byĩn duh mwah ?

What did the x-ray say?
Que montre la radio ?
Kuh mõntr laa raa-dyoh ?

Can I walk without a cane?
Est-ce que je peux marcher sans canne ?
Ehs-kuh zhuh puh maar-shey sãn kaan ?

Is the wheelchair necessary?
Le fauteuil roulant est-il nécessaire ?
Luh foh-tuh-y roo-lãn eh_teel ney-sey-sehr ?

Am I in the right area of the hospital?
Suis-je dans la bonne section de l'hôpital ?
Sweezh dãn laa bohn sehk-syõn duh loh-pee-taal ?

Where is the front desk receptionist?
Où est la réceptionniste ?
Oo eh laa rey-sehp-syoh-neest ?

I would like to go to a different waiting area.
Je veux aller dans une autre salle d'attente.
Zhuh vuh aa-ley dãn_zun_nohtr saal daa-tãnt.

Can I have a change of sheets, please?
Pouvez-vous changer les draps, s'il vous plaît ?
Poo-vey voo shãn-zhey ley drah seel voo pleh ?

Excuse me, what is your name?
Excusez-moi, quel est votre nom ?
Ehk-sku-zey mwah, kehl eh vohtr nõn ?

Who is the doctor in charge here?
C'est qui le médecin responsable ici ?
Sey kee luh med-sĩn rehs-põn-saabl ee-see ?

I need some assistance, please.
J'ai besoin d'aide, s'il vous plaît.
Zhey buh-zwĩn dehd seel voo pleh.

Will my recovery affect my ability to do work?
Ma convalescence va-t-elle affecter ma capacité à travailler ?
Maa kõn-vaa-leh-sãns vah-tehl aa-fehk-tey maa kaa-paa-see-tey aa traa-vah-yey ?

How long is the estimated recovery time?
Quelle est la durée de convalescence prévu ?
Kehl eh laa du-rey duh kõn-vaa-leh-sãns prey-vu ?

Is that all you can do for me? There has to be another option.
C'est tout ce que vous pouvez faire pour moi ? Il doit y avoir une autre option.
Sey too suh kuh voo poo-vey fehr poor mwah ? Eel dwah ee_yaa-vwahr un ohtr ohp-syõn.

I need help with motion sickness.
J'ai besoin d'aide pour le mal des transports.
Zhey buh-zwĩn dehd poor luh maal dey trãns-pohr.

I'm afraid of needles.
J'ai peur des aiguilles.
Zhey puhr dey_zey-gwee-y.

My gown is too small; I need another one.
Ma blouse est trop petite ; il m'en faut une autre.
Maa blooz eh troh puh-teet ; eel mãn foh un ohtr.

Can I have extra pillows?
Est-ce que je pourrais avoir des oreillers supplémentaires ?
Ehs-kuh zhuh poo-reh aa-vwahr dey_zoh-rey-yey su-pley-mãn-tehr ?

I need assistance getting to the bathroom.
J'ai besoin d'aide pour aller aux toilettes.
Zhey buh-zwĩn dehd poor_raa-ley oh twah-leht.

Hi, is the doctor in?
Bonjour, le docteur est là ?
Bõn-zhoor, luh dohk-tuhr eh lah ?

When should I schedule the next checkup?
Quand devrais-je programmer le prochain examen ?
Kãn duh-vrehzh proh-graa-mey luh proh-shĩn_nehg-zaa-mĩn ?

When can I have these stitches removed?
Quand est-ce que je peux faire enlever ces points de suture ?
Kãn_tehs kuh zhuh puh fehr ãn-luh-vey sey pwĩn duh su-tur ?

Do you have any special instructions while I'm in this condition?
Avez-vous des conseils particuliers tant que je suis dans cet état ?
Aa-vey voo dey kõn-seh-y paar-tee-ku-lyey tãn kuh zhuh swee dãn seht_tey-tah ?

ORDERING FOOD

Can I see the menu?
Puis-je voir le menu ?
Pweezh vwahr luh muh-nu ?

I'm really hungry. We should eat something soon.
J'ai vraiment faim. On devrait manger quelque chose bientôt.
Zhey vreh-mãn fĩn. Õn duh-vreh mãn-zhey kehl-kuh shohz byĩn-toh.

Can I take a look in the kitchen?
Puis-je jeter un coup d'œil dans la cuisine ?
Pweezh zhuh-tey ũn koo duh-y dãn laa kwee-zeen ?

Can we see the drink menu?
Pouvons-nous voir la carte des boissons ?
Poo-võn noo vwahr laa kaart dey bwah-sõn ?

When can we be seated?
Quand est-ce qu'on sera installé ?
Kãn_tehs kõn suh-rah ĩn-staa-ley ?

This is very tender and delicious.
C'est très tendre et délicieux.
Sey treh tãndr ey dey-lee-see-uh.

Do you serve alcohol?
Servez-vous de l'alcool ?
Sehr-vey voo duh laal-kohl ?

I'm afraid our party can't make it.
Notre partie ne peut pas vous rejoindre.
Nohtr paar-tee nuh puh pah voo ruh-zhwĩndr.

That room is reserved for us.
Cet espace nous est réservé.
Seht_teh-spahs noo_zeh-rey-zehr-vey.

Are there any seasonal favorites that you serve?
Y-a-t-il des produits saisonniers populaires que vous servez ?
Ee-yah teel dey proh-dwee seh-zoh-nyehr poh-pu-lehr kuh voo sehr-vey ?

Do you offer discounts for kids or seniors?
Proposez-vous des tarifs réduits pour les enfants ou les seniors ?
Proh-poh-zey voo dey taa-reef rey-dwee poor ley_zãn-fãn oo ley sey-nyohr ?

I would like it filleted.
Je le voudrais en filet.
Zhuh luh voo-dreh ãn fee-leh.

I would like to reserve a table for a party of four.
Je voudrais réserver une table pour un groupe de quatre personnes.
Zhuh voo-dreh rey-zehr-vey un taabl poor ũn groop duh kaatr pehr-sohn.

I would like to place the reservation under my name.
Je voudrais faire la réservation à mon nom.
Zhuh voo-dreh fehr laa rey-zehr-vaa-syõn aa mõn nõn.

What type of alcohol do you serve?
Quels types d'alcool servez-vous ?
Kehl teep daal-kohl sehr-vey voo ?

Do I need a reservation?
Est-ce que j'ai besoin d'une réservation ?
Eh-skuh zhey buh-zwĩn dun rey-zehr-vaa-syõn ?

What does it come with?
Ça vient avec quoi ?
Saa vyĩn aa-vehk kwah ?

What are the ingredients?
Quelles sont les ingrédients ?
Kel sõn ley_zĩn-grey-dee-ãn ?

What else does the chef put in the dish?
Qu'est-ce que le chef met d'autre dans le plat ?
Ke-skuh luh shehf meh dohtr dãn luh plah ?

I wonder which of these tastes better?
Je me demande lequel de ces deux a le meilleur goût ?
Zhuh muh duh-mãnd luh-kehl duh sey duh ah luh mey-uhr goo ?

That is incorrect. Our reservation was at noon.
C'est faux. Notre réservation était à midi.
Sey foh. Nohtr rey-zehr-vaa-syõn ey-tey aa mee-dee.

I would like red wine, please.
Je voudrais du vin rouge, s'il vous plaît.
Zhuh voo-dreh du vĩn roozh, seel voo pleh.

Can you choose the soup?
Pouvez-vous choisir la soupe ?
Poo-vey voo shwah-zeer laa soop?

What is the most popular dish here?
Quelle est le plat le plus apprécié ici ?
Kehl ey luh plah luh plus aa-prey-see-ey ee-see ?

What are the specials today?
Quels sont les plats du jour ?
Kehl sõn ley plah du zhoor ?

What are your appetizers?
Qu'est-ce que vous avez comme entrées ?
Keh-skuh voo_zaa-vey kohm ãn-trey ?

Please bring these out separately.
S'il vous plaît rammenez ceux-là séparément.
Seel voo pleh raa-muh-ney suh-lah sey-paa-rey-mãn.

Do we leave a tip?
Est-ce qu'on laisse un pourboire ?
Eh-skõn lehs ũn poor-bwahr ?

Are tips included with the bill?
Est-ce que le pourboire est inclu dans l'addition ?
Eh-skuh luh poor-bwahr eh_tĩn-klu dãn laa-dee-syõn ?

Split the bill, please.
Est-ce qu'on pourrait avoir la note séparée, s'il vous plaît ?
Eh-skõn poo-reh aa-vwahr laa noht sey-paa-rey seel-voo-pley ?

We are paying separately.
Nous allons payer séparément.
Noo_zaa-lõn pey-ey sey-paa-rey-mãn.

Is there an extra fee for sharing an entrée?
Y-a-t-il un tarif supplémentaire pour partager un plat ?
Yah teel ũn taa-reef su-pley-mãn-tehr poor paar-taa-zhey ũn plah ?

Is there a local specialty that you recommend?
Y-a-t-il une spécialité locale que vous pouvez me recommander ?
Yah teel un spey-see-aa-lee-tey loh-kaal kuh voo poo-vey muh ruh-koh-mãn-dey ?

This looks different from what I originally ordered.
Ceci n'a pas l'air d'être ce que j'ai commandé.
Suh-see nah pah lehr dehtr suh kuh zhey koh-mãn-dey.

Is this a self-serve buffet?
C'est un buffet à volonté ?
Sey_tûn bu-feh aa voh-lõn-tey ?

I want a different waiter.
Je veux un autre serveur.
Zhuh vuh ũn_nohtr sehr-vuhr.

Please move us to a different table.
Est-ce qu'on pourrait avoir une autre table, s'il-vous plait ?
Ehs-kõn poo-reh aa-vwahr u_nohtr taabl, seel voo pleh ?

Can we put two tables together?
Pouvons-nous joindre deux tables pour en faire une seule ?
Poo-võn noo zhwĩndr duh taabl poor ãn fehr un suhl ?

My spoon is dirty. Can I have another one?
Ma cuillère est sale. Puis-je avoir une autre ?
Maa kwee-ehr eh saal. Pweezh aa-vwahr un ohtr ?

We need more napkins, please.
Nous avons besoin de plus de serviettes, s'il vous plaît.
Noo_zaa-võn buh-zwĩn duh plus duh sehr-vee-eht, seel voo pleh.

I'm a vegetarian and don't eat meat.
Male: Je suis un végétarien, et je ne mange pas de viande.
Zhuh swee_zũn vey-zhey-taa-ryĩn, ey zhuh nuh mãnzh pah duh vee-ãnd.
Female: Je suis une végétarienne, et je ne mange pas de viande.
Zhuh swee_zun vey-zhey-taa-ryehn, ey zhuh nuh mãnzh pah duh vee-ãnd.

The table next to us is being too loud. Can you say something?
La table à côté fait trop de bruit. Pouvez-vous leur faire une remarque ?
Laa taabl aa koh-tey feh troh duh bru-ee. Poo-vey voo luhr fehr un ruh-maark ?

Someone is smoking in our non-smoking section.
Quelqu'un fume dans notre section non-fumeur.
Kehl-kũn fum dãn nohtr sehk-syõn nõn fu-muhr.

Please seat us in a booth.
On aimerait un box, s'il-vous plait.
Õn_nehm-reh ũn bohks, seel voo pleh.

Do you have any non-alcoholic beverages?
Avez-vous des boissons non-alcoolisées ?
Aa-vey voo dey bwah-sõn nõn aal-koh-lee-zey ?

Where is your bathroom?
Où se trouvent les toilettes ?
Oo suh troov ley twah-leht?

Are you ready to order?
Êtes-vous prêts à commander ?
Eht voo preh aa koh-mãn-dey ?

Five more minutes, please.
Cinq minutes de plus, s'il vous plaît.
Sĩnk mee-nut duh plus, seel voo pleh.

What time do you close?
À quelle heure vous fermez ?
Aa kehl uhr voo fehr-mey ?

Is there pork in this dish? I don't eat pork.
Y-a-t-il du porc dans ce plat ? Je ne mange pas de porc.
Yah teel du pohr dãn suh plah ? Zhuh nuh mãnzh pah duh pohr.

Do you have any dishes for vegans?
Avez-vous des plats végétaliens ?
Aa-vey voo dey plah vey-zhey-taa-lyĩn ?

Are these vegetables fresh?
Ces légumes sont-ils frais ?
Sey ley-gum sõn_teel freh ?

Have any of these vegetables been cooked in butter?
Est-ce que certains de ces légumes ont étés cuits avec du beurre ?
Ehs-kuh sehr-tĩn duh sey ley-gum õn_tey-tey kwee aa-vehk du buhr ?

Is this spicy?
C'est piquant ça ?
Sey pee-kãn sah ?

Is this sweet?
C'est sucré ça ?
Sey su-krey sah ?

I want more, please.
J'en veux plus, s'il vous plaît.
Zhãn vuh plus seel voo pleh.

I would like a dish containing these items.
Je voudrais un plat qui contient ces choses.
Zhuh voo-dreh ũn plah kee kõn-tyĩn sey shohz.

Can you make this dish light? Thank you.
Pouvez-vous faire ce plat plus léger ? Merci.
Poo-vey voo fehr suh plah plu ley-zhey ? Mehr-see.

Nothing else.
Rien de plus.
Ree-yĩn duh plus.

Please clear the plates.
S'il vous plaît, veuillez débarrasser les plats.
Seel voo pleh, vuh-yey dey-baa-raa-sey ley plah.

May I have a cup of soup?
Puis-je avoir une tasse de soupe ?
Pweezh aa-vwahr un tahs duh soop ?

Do you have any bar snacks?
Avez-vous des collations ?
Aa-vey voo dey koh-laa-syõn ?

Another round, please.
Une autre tournée de boissons, s'il vous plaît.
Un ohtr toor-ney duh bwah-sõn, seel voo pleh.

When is closing time for the bar?
À quelle heure le bar se ferme ?
Aa kehl uhr luh bahr suh fehrm ?

That was delicious!
C'était délicieux !
Sey-tey dey-lee-syuh !

Does this have alcohol in it?
Est-ce qu'il y a de l'alcool dans ça ?
Ehs-keel ee_yah duh laal-kohl dãn sah ?

Does this have nuts in it?
Est-ce qu'il y a des noix dans ça ?
Ehs-keel ee-ah dey nwah dãn sah ?

Is this gluten free?
Est-ce que c'est sans gluten ça ?
Ehs-kuh sey sãn glu-tĩn sah ?

Can I get this to go?
Puis-je avoir ça à emporter ?
Pweezh aa-vwahr sah aa ãm-pohr-tey ?

May I have a refill?
Puis-je avoir un autre ?
Pweezh aa-vwahr ũn_nohtr ?

Is this dish kosher?
Est-ce que ce plat est kascher ?
Ehs-kuh suh plah eh kaa-shehr ?

I would like to change my drink.
J'aimerais changer de boisson.
Zheh-muh-reh shãn-zhey duh bwah-sõn.

My coffee is cold. Could you please warm it up?
Mon café est froid. Pouvez-vous le réchauffer ?
Mõn kaa-fey eh frwah. Poo-vey voo luh rey-shoh-fey ?

Do you serve coffee?
Servez-vous le café ?
Sehr-vey voo luh kaa-fey ?

Can I please have cream in my coffee?
Puis-je avoir de la crème dans mon café ?
Pweezh aa-vwahr duh laa krehm dãn mõn kaa-fey ?

Please add extra sugar to my coffee.
S'il vous plaît mettez beaucoup de sucre dans mon café.
Seel voo pleh meh-tey boh-koo duh sukr dãn mõn kaa-fey.

I would like to have my coffee served black, no cream and no sugar.
J'aimerais un café noir, sans crème ni sucre.
Zheh-muh-reh ũn kaa-fey nwahr, sãn krehm nee sukr.

I would like to have decaffeinated coffee, please.
J'aimerais un café décaféiné, s'il vous plaît.
Zheh-muh-reh ũn kaa-fey dey-kaa-fey-ee-ney, seel voo pleh.

Do you serve coffee-flavored ice cream?
Servez-vous la crème glacée au café ?
Sehr-vey voo laa krehm glaa-sey oh kaa-fey ?

Please put my cream and sugar on the side so that I can add it myself.
S'il vous plaît laissez la crème et le sucre sur le côté pour que je puisse
l'ajouter moi-même.
*Seel voo pleh leh-sey laa krehm ey luh sukr sur luh koh-tey poor kuh zhuh
pwees laa-zhoo-tey mwah-mehm.*

I would like to order an iced coffee.
J'aimerais commander un café glacé.
Zheh-muh-reh koh-mãn-dey ũn kaa-fey glaa-sey.

I would like an espresso please.
J'aimerais un expresso, s'il vous plaît.
Zheh-muh-reh ũn_nehks-preh-soh, seel voo pleh.

Do you have 2% milk?
Avez-vous du lait demi-écrémé ?
Aa-vey voo du leh duh-mee ey-krey-mey ?

Do you serve soy milk?
Avez-vous du lait de soja ?
Aa-vey voo du leh duh soh-zhah ?

Do you have almond milk?
Avez-vous du lait d'amande ?
Aa-vey voo du leh daa-mãnd ?

Are there any alternatives to the milk you serve?
Avez-vous des substituts pour le lait ?
Aa-vey voo des sub-stee-tu poor luh leh ?

Please put the lemons for my tea on the side.
S'il vous plaît laissez le citron pour mon thé sur le côté.
Seel voo pleh leh-sey luh see-trõn poor mõn tey sur luh koh-tey.

No lemons with my tea, thank you.
Pas de citron avec mon thé, merci.
Pah duh see-trõn aa-vehk mõn tey, mehr-see.

Is your water from the tap?
Votre eau c'est de l'eau du robinet ?
Vohtr oh sey duh loh du roh-bee-neh ?

Sparkling water, please.
De l'eau gazeuse, s'il vous plaît.
Duh loh gah-zuhz, seel voo pleh.

Can I get a diet coke?
Puis-je avoir un coke diète ?
Pweezh aa-vwahr ũn kohk dee-eht ?

We're ready to order.
Nous sommes prêts à commander.
Noo sohm preh aa koh-mãn-dey.

Can we be seated over there instead?
Pouvons-nous s'asseoir là-bas à la place ?
Poo-võn noo saa-swahr laa-bah aa laa plaas ?

Can we have a seat outside?
Pouvons-nous s'asseoir dehors ?
Poo-võn noo saa-swahr duh-ohr ?

Please hold the salt.
S'il vous plaît n'ajoutez pas de sel.
Seel voo pleh naa-zhoo-tey pah duh sehl.

This is what I would like for my main course.
J'aimerais ça comme plat principal.
Zheh-muh-reh sah kohm plah prĩn-see-paal.

I would like the soup instead of the salad.
J'aimerais avoir la soupe à la place de la salade.
Zheh-muh-reh aa-vwahr laa soop aa laa plaas duh laa saa-laad.

I'll have the chicken risotto.
Je prendrais le risotto au poulet.
Zhuh prãn-dreh luh ree-zoh-toh oh poo-leh.

Can I change my order?
Puis-je changer ma commande ?
Pweezh shãn-zhey maa koh-mãnd ?

Do you have a kids' menu?
Avez-vous un menu enfant ?
Aa-vey voo ũn muh-nu ãn-fãn ?

When does the lunch menu end?
À quelle heure vous arrêtez de servir le menu de midi ?
Aa kehl uhr voo_zaa-reh-tey duh sehr-veer luh muh-nu duh mee-dee ?

When does the dinner menu start?
À quelle heure vous commencez à servir le menu du dîner ?
Aa kehl uhr voo koh-mãn-sey aa sehr-veer luh muh-nu duh dee-ney ?

Do you have any recommendations from the menu?
Pouvez-vous nous faire des recommendations du menu ?
Poo-vey voo noo fehr dey ruh-koh-mãn-daa-syõn du muh-nu ?

I would like to place an off-menu order.
J'aimerais commander quelque chose qui n'est pas sur le menu.
Zheh-muh-reh koh-mãn-dey kehl-kuh shohz kee neh pah sur luh muh-nu.

Can we see the dessert menu?
Pouvons-nous voir la carte de dessert ?
Poo-võn noo vwahr laa kaart duh dey-sehr ?

Is this available sugar-free?
Est-ce que ceci est disponible sans sucre ?
Ehs-kuh suh-see eh dee-spoh-neebl sãn sukr ?

May we have the bill, please?
Pouvons-nous avoir l'addition, s'il vous plaît ?
Poo-võn noo aa-vwahr laa-dee-syõn seel voo pleh ?

Where do we pay?
Où pouvons-nous payer ?
Oo poo-võn noo pey-ey ?

Hi, we are with the party of Isaac.
Salut, nous sommes avec le groupe d'Isaac.
Saa-lu, noo sohm_zaa-vehk luh groop dee-zaak.

We haven't made up our minds yet on what to order. Can we have a few more minutes, please?
On n'a pas encore décidé quoi commander. On peut avoir quelques minutes de plus, s'il vous plaît ?
Õn_nah pah_zãn-kahr dey-see-dey kwah koh-mãn-dey. Õn puh aa-vwahr kel-kuh mee-nut duh plus, seel voo pleh ?

Waiter!
Monsieur !
Muh-syuh !

Waitress!
Madame !
Maa-daam !

I'm still deciding, come back to me, please.
Je n'ai pas encore choisi, vous pouvez revenir, s'il vous plaît ?
Zhuh ney pah_zãn-kahr shwah-zee, voo poo-vez ruh-vuh-neer, seel voo pleh ?

Can we have a pitcher of that?
On peut avoir une carafe de cela ?
Õn puh aa-vwahr un kaa-raaf duh suh-lah ?

This is someone else's meal.
C'est le repas de quelqu'un d'autre.
Sey luh ruh-pah duh kehl-kũn dohtr.

Can you please heat this up a little more?
Pouvez-vous réchauffer ceci un peu plus ?
Poo-vey voo rey-shoh-fey suh-see ũn puh plus ?

I'm afraid I didn't order this.
Ceci n'est pas ce que j'ai commandé.
Suh-see neh pah skuh zhey koh-mãn-dey.

The same thing again, please.
Encore la même chose, s'il vous plaît.
Ãn-kahr laa mehm shohz, seel voo pleh.

Can we have another bottle of wine?
Pouvons-nous avoir une autre bouteille de vin ?
Poo-võn noo aa-vwahr un ohtr boo-teh-y duh vĩn ?

That was perfect, thank you!
C'était parfait, merci !
Sey-teh paar-feh, mehr-see !

Everything was good.
Tout était très bon.
Too_tey-teh treh bõn.

Can we have the bill?
Pouvons-nous avoir l'addition ?
Poo-võn noo aa-vwahr laa-dee-syõn ?

I'm sorry, but this bill is incorrect.
Désolé, mais cette addition n'est pas exacte.
Dey-zoh-ley, meh seht aa-dee-syõn neh pah eg-zaakt.

Can I have clean cutlery?
Puis-je avoir un couvert propre ?
Pweezh aa-vwahr ũn koo-vehr prohpr ?

Can we have more napkins?
Pouvons-nous avoir plus de serviettes ?
Poo-võn noo aa-vwahr plus duh sehr-vee-eht ?

May I have another straw?
Puis-je avoir une autre paille ?
Pweezh aa-vwahr un ohtr pah-y ?

What sides can I have with that?
Quels sont les choix d'accompagnement ?
Kehl sõn ley shwah daa-kõn-paa-nyuh-mãn ?

Excuse me, but this is overcooked.
Pardonnez-moi, mais ceci est trop cuit.
Paar-doh-ney mwah, meh suh-see eh troh kwee.

May I talk to the chef?
Puis-je parler au chef ?
Pweezh paar-ley oh shehf ?

We have booked a table for fifteen people.
Nous avons réservé une table pour quinze personnes.
Noo_zaa-võn rey-zehr-vey un taabl poor kĩnz pehr-sohn.

Are there any tables free?
Y-a-t-il des tables de libres ?
Ee-yah teel dey taabl duh leebr ?

I would like one beer, please.
J'aimerais avoir une bière, s'il vous plaît.
Zheh-muh-reh aa-vwahr un byehr, seel voo pleh.

Can you add ice to this?
Pouvez-vous mettre de la glace dedans ?
Poo-vey voo mehtr duh laa glaas duh-dãn ?

I would like to order a dark beer.
J'aimerais commander une bière brune.
Zheh-muh-reh koh-mãn-dey un byehr brun.

Do you have any beer from the tap?
Avez-vous des bières pression ?
Aa-vey voo dey byehr preh-syõn ?

How expensive is your champagne?
Quel est le prix de votre champagne ?
Kehl eh luh pree duh vohtr shãn-paa-ny ?

Enjoy your meal.
Bon appétit !
Boh_naa-pey-tee !

I want this.
Je veux ça.
Zhuh vuh sah.

Please cook my meat well done.
S'il vous plaît faites bien cuire la viande.
Seel voo pleh feht byîn kuir laa vee-ãnd.

Please cook my meat medium rare.
S'il vous plaît faites cuire la viande à point.
Seel voo pleh feht kuir laa vee-ãnd aa pwĩn.

Please prepare my meat rare.
S'il vous plaît préparez la viande saignante.
Seel voo pleh prey-paa-rey laa vee-ãnd seh-nyãnt.

What type of fish do you serve?
Quels genres de poissons servez-vous ?
Kehl zhãnr duh pwah-sõn sehr-vey voo ?

Can I make a substitution with my meal?
Puis-je faire une substitution dans mon repas ?
Pweezh fehr un sub-stee-tu-syõn dãn mõn ruh-pah ?

Do you have a booster seat for my child?
Avez-vous une chaise réhausseur pour mon enfant ?
Aa-vey voo un shehz rey-oh-suhr poor mõn_nãn-fãn ?

Call us when you get a table.
Appelez-nous lorsque vous obtenez une table.
Aa-puh-ley noo lohr-skuh voo_zohb-tuh-ney un taabl.

Is this a non-smoking section?
Est-ce que cette section est non-fumeur ?
Ehs-kuh seht sehk-syõn eh nõn-fu-muhr ?

We would like to be seated in the smoking section.
Nous aimerions s'asseoir dans la section fumeur.
Noo_zeh-muh-ree-õn saa-swahr dãn laa sehk-syõn fu-muhr.

This meat tastes funny.

Cette viande a un goût bizarre.

Seht vee-ãnd ah ũn goo bee-zahr.

More people will be joining us later.

Il y a d'autres personnes qui vont nous rejoindre plus tard.

Eel ee_yah dohtr pehr-sohn kee võn noo ruh-zhwĩndr plu tahr.

TRANSPORTATION

Where's the train station?
Où se trouve la gare ?
Oo suh troov laa gahr ?

How much does it cost to get to this address?
Combien ça coûte pour aller à cette adresse ?
Kõm-byĩn saa koot poor aa-ley aa seht aa-drehs ?

What type of payment do you accept?
Quelles modes de paiement acceptez-vous ?
Kehl mohd duh pey-mãn aak-sehp-tey voo ?

Do you have first-class tickets available?
Avez-vous des billets de première classe disponibles ?
Aa-vey voo dey bee-yeh duh pruh-myehr klahs dees-poh-neebl ?

What platform do I need to be on to catch this train?
Sur quel quai je dois être pour prendre ce train ?
Sur kehl key zhuh dwah ehtr poor prãndr suh trĩn ?

Are the roads paved in this area?
Les routes sont-elles goudronnées dans cette région ?
Ley root sõn_tehl goo-droh-ney dãn seht rey-zhyõn ?

Where are the dirt roads, and how do I avoid them?
Où sont les routes de terre, et comment puis-je les éviter ?
Oo sõn ley root duh tehr, ey koh-mãn pweezh ley_zey-vee-tey ?

Are there any potholes I need to avoid?
Y-a-t-il des nids de poule que je dois éviter ?
Ee-yah teel dey nee duh pool kuh zhuh dwah ey-vee-tey ?

How fast are you going?
Vous faites quelle vitesse ?
Voo feht kehl vee-tehs ?

Do I need to put my emergency blinkers on?
Est-ce que je devrais allumer mes feux de détresse ?
Ehs-kuh zhuh duh-vreh aa-lu-mey mey fuh duh dey-trehs ?

Make sure to use the right turn signals.
N'oubliez pas d'utiliser votre indicateur droit.
Noo-blee-ey pah du-tee-lee-zey vohtr ĩn-dee-kaa-tuhr drwaa.

We need a good mechanic.
Nous avons besoin d'un bon mécanicien.
Noo_zaa-võn buh-zwĩn dũn bõn mey-kaa-nee-syĩn.

Can we get a push?
Pouvez-vous nous aider à pousser la voiture ?
Poo-vey voo noo_zey-dey aa poo-sey laa vwah-tur ?

I have to call the towing company to move my car.
Je dois appeler l'entreprise de remorquage pour déplacer ma voiture.
Zhuh dwah aa-puh-ley lãn-truh-preez duh ruh-mohr-kaazh poor dey-plaa-sey maa vwah-tur.

Make sure to check the battery and spark plugs for any problems.
N'oubliez pas d'inspecter la batterie et les bougies pour d'éventuels problèmes.
Noo-blee-ey pah dĩn-spehk-tey laa baa-tree ey ley boo-zhee poor dey-vãn-tu-ehl proh-blehm.

Check the oil level.
Vérifiez le niveau d'huile.
Vey-ree-fee-ey luh nee-voh dweel.

I need to notify my insurance company.
Je dois informer ma compagnie d'assurance.
Zhuh dwah_zĩn-fohr-mey maa kõn-paa-nyee daa-su-rãns.

When do I pay the taxi driver?
Quand est-ce que je paie le chauffeur de taxi ?
Kãn_tehs-kuh zhuh peh-y luh shoh-fuhr duh taak-see ?

Please take me to the nearest train station.
S'il vous plaît prenez-moi à la gare la plus proche.
Seel voo pleh pruh-ney mwah aa laa gahr laa plu prohsh.

How long does it take to get to this address?
Combien de temps il faut pour se rendre à cette adresse ?
Kõm-byĩn duh tãn eel foh poor suh rãndr aa seht aa-drehs ?

Can you stop here, please?
Arrêtez-vous ici, s'il vous plaît.
Aa-reh-tey voo ee-see seel voo pleh.

You can drop me off anywhere around here.
Vous pouvez me déposer n'importe où dans ce coin.
Voo poo-vey muh dey-poh-zey nĩn-pohrt oo dãn suh kwĩn.

Is there a charge for extra passengers?
Y-a-t-il un tarif pour des passagers supplémentaires ?
Ee-ya teel ũn taa-reef poor dey pah-saa-zhey su-pley-mãn-tehr ?

What is the condition of the road? Is it safe to travel there?
Quelle est la condition de la route ? Est-ce qu'on peut voyager en sécurité là-bas ?
Kehl eh laa kõn-dee-syõn duh laa root ? Ehs-kõn puh vwah-yaa-zhey ãn sey-ku-ree-tey laa-bah ?

Take me to the emergency room.
Prenez-moi à la salle d'urgence.
Pruh-ney mwah aa laa saal dur-zhãns.

Take me to the embassy.
Prenez-moi à l'ambassade.
Pruh-ney mwah aa lãm-baa-saad.

I want to travel around the country.
Je veux faire le tour du pays.
Zhuh vuh fehr luh toor du pey-ee.

Is this the right side of the road?
Est-ce le bon côté de la route ?
Ehs luh bõn koh-tey duh laa root ?

77

My car broke down, please help!
Ma voiture est en panne, s'il vous plaît aidez-moi !
Maa vwah-tur eh_tãn paan, seel voo pleh ey-dey mwah !

Can you help me change my tire?
Pouvez-vous m'aider à changer mon pneu ?
Poo-vey voo mey-dey aa shãn-zhey mõn pnuh ?

Where can I get a rental car?
Où puis-je louer une voiture ?
Oo pweezh loo-ey un vwah-tur ?

Please take us to the hospital.
S'il vous plaît prenez-nous à l'hôpital.
Seel voo pleh pruh-ney noo aa loh-pee-taal.

Is that the car rental office?
C'est ça le bureau de location de voiture ?
Sey sah luh bu-roh duh loh-kaa-syõn duh vwah-tur ?

May I have a price list for your fleet?
Puis-je voir les prix de vos voitures ?
Pweezh vwahr ley pree duh voh vwah-tur ?

Can I get insurance on this rental car?
Puis-je souscrire une assurance pour cette voiture de location ?
Pweezh soo-skreer un aa-su-rãns poor seht vwah-tur duh loh-kaa-syõn ?

How much is the car per day?
Combien la voiture coûte par jour ?
Kõm-byĩn laa vwah-tur koot paar zhoor ?

How many kilometers can I travel with this car?
Combien de kilomètres puis-je voyager avec cette voiture ?
Kõm-byĩn duh kee-loh-mehtr pweezh vwah-yaa-zhey aa-vehk seht vwah-tur ?

I would like maps of the region if you have them.
J'aimerais avoir des cartes de la région si vous en avez.
Zheh-muh-reh aa-vwahr dey kaart duh laa rey-zhyõn see vou_zãn_naa-vey.

When I am done with the car, where do I return it?
Où est-ce que je rends la voiture à la fin de mon voyage ?
Oo ehs-kuh zhuh rãn laa vwah-tur aa laa fïn duh mõn vwah-yaazh ?

Is this a standard or automatic transmission?
Est-ce une boîte de vitesse manuelle ou automatique ?
Ehs un bwaht duh vee-tehs maa-nu-ehl oo oh-toh-maa-teek ?

Is this car gas-efficient? How many kilometers per liter?
Est-ce un véhicule économe en carburant ? Quel est le kilométrage par litre ?
Ehs ũn vey-ee-kul ey-koh-nohm ãn kaar-bu-rãn ? Kehl eh luh kee-loh-mey-trazh paar leetr ?

Where is the spare tire stored?
Où se trouve le pneu de secours ?
Oo suh troov luh pnuh duh suh-koor ?

Are there places around the city that are difficult to drive?
Y-a-t-il des lieux dans la ville où c'est difficile de conduire ?
Ee-yah-teel dey lyuh dãn laa veel oo sey dee-fee-seel duh kõn-dweer ?

At what time of the day is the traffic the worst?
À quelle heure de la journée l'encombrement devient le plus grave ?
Aa kehl uhr duh laa zhoor-ney lãn-kõn-bruh-mãn duh-vyïn luh plu graav ?

We can't park right here.
On ne peut pas se garer ici.
Õn nuh puh pah suh gah-rey ee-see.

What is the speed limit?
Quelle est la limite de vitesse ?
Kehl eh laa lee-meet duh vee-tehs ?

Keep the change.
Gardez la monnaie.
Gaar-dey laa moh-neh.

Now let's get off here.
Débarquons ici.
Dey-baar-kõn ee-see.

Where is the train station?
Où est la gare ?
Oo eh laa gaar ?

Is the bus stop nearby?
Est-ce que l'arrêt de bus est proche ?
Ehs-kuh laa-reh duh bus eh prohsh ?

When does the bus run?
À quelle heure le bus marche ?
Aa kehl uhr luh bus maarsh ?

Where do I go to catch a taxi?
Où est-ce que je peux prendre un taxi ?
Oo ehs-kuh zhuh puh prãndr ũn taak-see ?

Does the train go to the north station?
Est-ce que le train va à la gare du nord ?
Ehs-kuh luh trĩn vah aa laa gahr du nohr ?

Where do I go to purchase tickets?
Où je dois aller pour acheter des billets ?
Oo zhuh dwah aa-ley poor aa-shuh-tey dey bee-eh ?

How much is a ticket to the north?
Combien coûte un billet pour aller au nord ?
Kõm-byĩn koot ũn bee-eh poor aa-ley oh nohr ?

What is the next stop along this route?
Quel est le prochain arrêt sur cette route ?
Kehl eh luh proh-shĩn_naa-reh sur seht root ?

Can I have a ticket to the north?
Puis-je avoir un billet pour aller au nord ?
Pweezh aa-vwahr ũn bee-eh poor aa-ley oh nohr ?

Where is my designated platform?
Où se trouve mon quai désigné ?
Oo suh troov mõn keh dey-zee-nyey ?

Where do I place my luggage?
Où devrais-je mettre ma valise ?
Oo duh-vrehzh mehtr maa vaa-leez ?

Are there any planned closures today?
Y-a-t-il des fermetures prévues aujourd'hui ?
Ee-yah-teel dey fehr-muh-tur prey-vu oh-zhoor-dwee ?

Where are the machines that disperse tickets?
Où sont les guichets automatiques de billets ?
Oo sõn ley gee-shey oh-toh-maa-teek duh bee-eh ?

Does this car come with insurance?
Cette voiture vient-elle avec l'assurance ?
Seht vwah-tur vyĩn_tehl aa-vehk laa-su-rãns ?

May I have a timetable, please?
Puis-je avoir une copie de l'horaire des trains, s'il vous plaît ?
Pweezh aa-vwahr un koh-pee duh loh-rehr dey trĩn, seel voo pleh ?

How often do trains come to this area?
Quelle est la fréquence d'arrêts des trains ici ?
Kehl eh laa frey-kãns daa-reh dey trĩn ee-see ?

Is the train running late?
Est-ce que le train est en retard ?
Ehs-kuh luh trĩn eh_tãn ruh-tahr ?

Has the train been cancelled?
Est-ce que le train a été annulé ?
Ehs-kuh luh trĩn ah ey-tey aa-nu-ley ?

Is this seat available?
Est-ce que cette place est libre ?
Ehs-kuh seht plaas eh leebr ?

Do you mind if I sit here?
Je peux m'asseoir ici ?
Zhuh puh maa-swahr ee-see ?

I've lost my ticket.
J'ai perdu mon billet.
Zhey pehr-du mõn bee-eh.

Excuse me, this is my stop.
Pardonnez-moi, c'est mon arrêt ici.
Paar-doh-ney mwah, sey mõn_naa-reh ee-see.

Can you please open the window?
Pouvez-vous ouvrir la fenêtre ?
Poo-vey voo oo-vreer laa fuh-nehtr ?

Is smoking allowed in the car?
Est-ce que c'est permis de fumer dans la voiture ?
Ehs-kuh sey pehr-mee duh fu-mey dãn laa vwah-tur ?

Wait, my luggage is still on board!
Attendez, mes bagages sont encore à bord !
Aa-tãn-dey, mey baa-gaazh sõn ãn-kahr aa bahr !

Where can I get a map?
Où puis-je obtenir une carte ?
Oo pweezh ohb-tuh-neer un kaart ?

What zone is this?
C'est quelle zone ça ?
Sey kehl zohn sah ?

Please be careful of the gap!
S'il vous plaît faites attention à l'intervalle !
Seel voo pleh feht aa-tãn-syõn aa lĩn-tehr-vaal !

I am about to run out of gas.
Je vais bientôt être en panne d'essence.
Zhuh veh byĩn-toh ehtr ãn paan deh-sãns.

My tank is halfway full.
Mon réservoir est à moitié rempli.
Mõn rey-zehr-vwahr eh_taa mwah-tee-ey rãn-plee.

What type of gas does this car take?
Quel genre d'essence cette voiture utilise ?
Kehl zhãnr deh-sãns seht vwah-tur u-tee-leez ?

There is gas leaking out of my car.
J'ai une fuite d'essence dans ma voiture.
Zhey un fweet deh-sãns dãn maa vwah-tur.

Fill up the tank.
Remplissez le réservoir.
Rãm-plee-sey luh rey-zehr-vwahr.

There is no more gas in my car.
Il n'y a plus d'essence dans ma voiture.
Eel nee ah plu deh-sãns dãn maa vwah-tur.

Where can I find the nearest gas station?
Où se trouve la station-service la plus proche ?
Oo suh troov laa staa-syõn sehr-vees laa plu prohsh ?

The engine light for my car is on.
Le témoin de vérification moteur de ma voiture est allumé.
Luh tey-mwĩn duh vey-ree-fee-kaa-syõn moh-tuhr duh maa vwah-tur eh_taa-lu-mey.

Do you mind if I drive?
Ça ne vous dérange pas si je conduis ?
Saa nuh voo dey-rãnzh pah see zhuh kõn-dwee ?

Please get in the back seat.
S'il vous plaît asseyez-vous derrière.
Seel voo pleh aa-sey-ey voo deh-ree-ehr.

Let me get my bags out before you leave.
Laissez-moi sortir mes bagages avant que vous partiez.
Leh-sey mwah sohr-teer mey baa-gaazh aa-vãn kuh voo paar-tee-ey.

The weather is bad, please drive slowly.
Le temps est mauvais, s'il vous plaît conduisez doucement.
Luh tãn eh moh-veh, seel voo pleh kõn-dwee-zey doo-smãn.

Our vehicle isn't equipped to travel there.
Notre véhicule n'est pas équipé pour voyager là-bas.
Nohtr vey-ee-kul neh pah_zey-kee-pey poor vwah-yaa-zhey laa-bah.

One ticket to the north, please.
Un billet au nord, s'il vous plaît.
Ũn bee-eh oh nohr, seel voo pleh.

If you get lost, call me.
Si vous vous perdez, appelez-moi.
See voo voo pehr-dey, aa-puh-ley mwah.

That bus is overcrowded. I will wait for the next one.
Le bus est surchargé. Je vais attendre le prochain.
Luh bus eh sur-shaar-zhey. Zhuh veh aa-tãndr luh proh-shĩn.

Please, take my seat.
S'il vous plaît, prenez ma place.
Seel voo pleh, pruh-ney maa plaas.

Ma'am, I think your stop is coming up.
Madame, je crois qu'on s'approche de votre arrêt.
Maa-daam, zhuh krwa kõn saa-prohsh duh vohtr aa-reh.

Wake me up when we get to our destination.
Réveillez-moi lorsqu'on arrive à notre destination.
Rey-veh-yey mwah lohr-skõn_naa-reev aa nohtr dehs-tee-naa-syõn.

I would like to purchase a travel pass for the entire day.
J'aimerais acheter une carte de transport pour la journée entière.
Zheh-muh-reh aa-shuh-tey un kaart duh trãn-spohr poor laa zhoor-ney ãn-tyehr.

Would you like to swap seats with me?
Voulez-vous échanger de places avec moi ?
Voo-ley voo ey-shãn-zhey duh plaas aa-vehk mwah ?

I want to sit with my family.
Je veux m'asseoir avec ma famille.
Zhuh vuh maa-swahr aa-vehk maa faa-mee-y.

I would like a window seat for this trip.

J'aimerais un siège hublot pour ce voyage.

Zheh-muh-reh ũn syehzh u-bloh poor suh vwah-yaazh.

RELIGIOUS QUESTIONS

Where can I go to pray?
Où puis-je aller pour prier ?
Oo pweezh aa-ley poor pree-ey ?

What services does your church offer?
Quels services sont offerts par votre église ?
Kehl sehr-vees sõn_toh-fehr paar vohtr ey-gleez ?

Are you non-denominational?
Êtes-vous interconfessionnel ?
Eht voo ĩn-tehr-kõn-feh-syoh-nehl ?

Is there a shuttle to your church?
Y-a-t-il une navette pour aller à votre église ?
Ee-ya teel un naa-veht poor aa-ley aa vohtr ey-gleez ?

How long does church last?
C'est quoi la durée du service ?
Sey kwah laa du-rey du sehr-vees ?

Where is your bathroom?
Où se trouve votre salle de bain ?
Oo suh troov vohtr saal duh bĩn ?

What should I wear to your services?
Comment je devrais m'habiller pour assister à vos services ?
Koh-mãn zhuh duh-vreh maa-bee-yey poor aa-sees-tey aa voh sehr-vees ?

Where is the nearest Catholic church?
Où se trouve l'église catholique la plus proche ?
Oo suh troov ley-gleez kaa-toh-leek laa plu prohsh ?

Where is the nearest mosque?
Où se trouve la mosquée la plus proche ?
Oo suh troov laa mohs-key laa plu prohsh ?

Does your church perform weddings?
Est-ce que votre église éffectue les célébrations de mariage ?
Ehs-kuh vohtr ey-gleez ey-fehk-tu ley sey-ley-braa-syõn duh maa-ree-aazh ?

Who is getting married?
Qui se marie ?
Kee suh maa-ree ?

Will our marriage license be legal if we leave the country?
Est-ce que notre contrat de mariage sera valable à l'étranger ?
Ehs-kuh nohtr kõn-trah duh maa-ree-aazh suh-rah vaa-laabl aa ley-trãn-zhey ?

Where do we get our marriage license?
Où pouvons-nous procurer notre contrat de mariage ?
Oo poo-võn noo proh-ku-rey nohtr kõn-trah duh maa-ree-aazh ?

What is the charge for marrying us?
Quels sont les frais pour se marier ?
Kehl sõn ley freh poor suh maa-ree-ey ?

Do you handle same-sex marriage?
Faites-vous les mariages entre des personnes de même sexe ?
Feht voo ley maa-ree-aazh ãntr dey pehr-sohn duh mehm sehks ?

Please gather here to pray.
S'il vous plaît réunissez-vous ici pour prier.
Seel voo pleh rey-u-nee-sey voo ee-see poor pree-ey.

I would like to lead a sermon.
J'aimerais prêcher un sermon.
Zheh-muh-reh preh-shey ũn sehr-mõn.

I would like to help with prayer.
J'aimerais assister avec la prière.
Zheh-muh-reh aa-sees-tey aa-vehk laa pree-ehr.

How should I dress before arriving?
Comment je devrais m'habiller avant d'arriver ?
Koh-mãn zhuh duh-vreh maa-bee-yey aa-vãn daa-ree-vey ?

What are your rules?
Quelles sont vos règles ?
Kehl sõn voh rehgl ?

Are cell phones allowed in your building?
Les portables sont-ils permis dans votre bâtiment ?
Ley pohr-taabl sõn_teel pehr-mee dãn vohtr bah-tee-mãn ?

I plan on bringing my family this Sunday.
Je compte emmener ma famille avec moi ce dimanche.
Zhuh kõnt ah-muh-ney maa faa-mee-y aa-vehk mwah suh dee-mãnsh.

Do you accept donations?
Acceptez-vous les dons ?
Aak-sehp-tey voo ley dõn ?

I would like to offer my time to your cause.
J'aimerais offrir de mon temps comme bénévole pour votre cause.
Zheh-muh-reh oh-freer duh mõn tãn kohm bey-ney-vohl poor vohtr kohz.

What book should I be reading from?
De quelle livre je devrais lire ?
Duh kehl leevr zhuh duh-vreh leer ?

Do you have a gift store?
Avez-vous une boutique de cadeaux ?
Aa-vey voo un boo-teek duh caa-doh ?

EMERGENCY

I need help over here!
J'ai besoin d'aide ici !
Zhey buh-zwĩn dehd ee-see !

I'm lost, please help me.
Je suis perdu, s'il vous plaît aidez-moi.
Zhuh swee pehr-du, seel voo pleh ey-dey mwah.

Someone call the police!
Appelez la police !
Aa-puh-ley laa poh-lees !

Is there a lawyer who speaks English?
Y-a-t-il un avocat qui parle l'anglais ?
Ee-yah teel ũn_naa-voh-kah kee paarl lãn-gleh ?

Please help, my car doesn't work.
S'il vous plaît aidez-moi, ma voiture est en panne.
Seel voo pleh eh-dey mwah, maa vwah-tur eh_tãn paan.

There was a collision!
Il y a eu un accident !
Eel ee ah u ũn_naak-see-dãn !

Call an ambulance!
Appelez une ambulance !
Aa-puh-lez un ãm-bu-lãns !

Am I under arrest?
Suis-je en état d'arrestation ?
Sweezh ãn_ney-tah daa-rehs-taa-syõn ?

I need an interpreter, this is an emergency!
J'ai besoin d'un interprète, c'est une urgence !
Zhey buh-zwĩn dũn_nĩn-tehr-preht, seh_tun ur-zhãns !

My back hurts.
Mon dos me fait mal.
Mõn doh muh feh maal.

Is there an American consulate here?
Y-a-t-il un consulat américain ici ?
Ee-yah teel ũn kõn-su-lah aa-mey-ree-kĩn ee-see ?

I'm sick and don't feel too well.
Je suis malade, et je ne me sens pas bien.
Zhuh swee maa-laad, ey zhuh nuh muh sãn pah byĩn.

Is there a pharmacy where I can get medicine?
Y-a-t-il une pharmacie où je peux acheter des médicaments ?
Ee-yah teel un faar-maa-see oo zhuh puh aa-shuh-tey dey mey-dee-kaa-mãn ?

I need a doctor immediately.
J'ai besoin d'un médecin immédiatement.
Zhey buh-zwĩn dũn meyd-sĩn ee-mey-dyaat-mãn.

I have a tooth missing.
Il me manque une dent.
Eel muh mãnk un dãn.

Please! Someone bring my child to me!
S'il vous plaît ! Quelqu'un rammenez-moi mon enfant !
Seel voo pleh ! Kehl-kũn raa-muh-ney mwah mõn_nãn-fãn !

Where does it hurt?
Où avez-vous mal ?
Oo aa-vey voo maal ?

Hold on to me!
Tenez-moi !
Tuh-ney mwah !

There's an emergency!
Il y a une urgence !
Eel ee ah un ur-zhãns !

I need a telephone to call for help.
J'ai besoin d'un téléphone pour appeler du secours.
Zhey buh-zwĩn dũn tey-ley-fohn poor aa-puh-ley du suh-koor.

My nose is bleeding.
Mon nez saigne.
Mõn ney seh-ny.

I twisted my ankle.
Je me suis tordu la cheville.
Zhuh muh swee tohr-du laa shuh-vee-y.

I don't feel so good.
Je ne me sens pas bien.
Zhuh nuh muh sãn pah byĩn.

Don't move, please.
S'il vous plaît ne bougez pas.
Seel voo pleh nuh boo-zhey pah.

Hello operator, can I place a collect call?
Salut, est-ce que je peux faire un appel à frais virés ?
Saa-lu, ehs-kuh zhuh puh fehr ũn_naa-pehl aa freh vee-rey ?

I'll get a doctor for you.
Je vais te chercher un médecin.
Zhuh veh tuh shehr-shey ũn mehd-sĩn.

Please hold my passports for a while.
S'il vous plaît tenez mes passeports pendant un moment.
Seel voo pleh tuh-ney mey paas-pohr pãn-dãn ũn moh-mãn.

I lost my wallet.
J'ai perdu mon portefeuille.
Zhey pehr-du mõn pohr-tuh-fuh-y.

I have a condition! Please check my wallet.
J'ai une condition médicale ! S'il vous plaît regardez dans mon portefeuille.
Zhey un kõn-dee-syõn mey-dee-kaal ! Seel voo pleh ruh-gaar-dey dãn mõn pohr-tuh-fuh-y.

91

My wife is in labor, please help!
Ma femme accouche, s'il vous plaît aidez-nous !
Maa faam aa-koosh, seel voo pleh eh-dey noo !

I would like to talk to my lawyer.
J'aimerais parler à mon avocat.
Zheh-muh-reh paar-ley aa mõn_naa-voh-kah.

It's an earthquake!
C'est un tremblement de terre !
Sey_tũn trãm-bluh-mãn duh tehr !

Get under the desk and protect your head.
Mettez-vous en-dessous du bureau et protégez votre tête.
Muh-tey voo ãn duh-soo du bu-roh ey proh-tey-zhey vohtr teht.

How can I help you?
Comment puis-je vous aider ?
Koh-mãn pweezh voo_zeh-dey ?

Everyone, he needs help!
Tout le monde, il a besoin d'aide !
Too luh mõnd, eel ah buh-zwĩn dehd !

Yes, help me get an ambulance.
Oui, aidez-moi à appeler une ambulance.
Wee, eh-dey mwah aa aa-puh-ley un ãm-bu-lãns.

Thank you, but I am fine. Please don't help me.
Merci, mais ça va. S'il vous plaît ne m'aidez pas.
Mehr-see meh saa vah. Seel voo pleh nuh meh-dey pah.

I need help carrying this injured person.
J'ai besoin d'aide à porter cette personne blessée.
Zhey buh-zwĩn dehd aa pohr-tey seht pehr-sohn bleh-sey.

TECHNOLOGY

What is the country's official website?
Quel est le site officiel du pays ?
Kehl eh luh seet oh-fee-see-ehl du pey-ee ?

Do you know the name of a good wi-fi café?
Connaissez-vous le nom d'un bon cybercafé ?
Koh-neh-sey voo luh nõn dũn bõn see-behr-kaa-fey ?

Do you have any experience with computers?
Avez-vous de l'expérience avec les ordinateurs ?
Aa-vey voo duh lehks-pey-ree-ãns aa-vehk ley_zohr-dee-naa-tuhr ?

How well do you know Apple products?
Quel est votre niveau de connaissance des produits Apple ?
Kehl eh vohtr nee-voh duh koh-neh-sãns dey proh-dwee aapl ?

What kind of work did you do with computers?
Quel genre de travail avez-vous fait avec les ordinateurs ?
Kehl zhãnr duh traa-vah-y aa-vey voo feh aa-vehk ley_ zohr-dee-naa-tuhr ?

Are you a programmer?
Êtes-vous un programmeur ?
Eht voo ũn proh-graa-muhr ?

Are you a developer?
Êtes-vous un développeur ?
Eht voo ũn dey-vloh-puhr ?

I want to use this computer instead of that one.
Je veux utiliser cet ordinateur au lieu de celui-là.
Zhuh vuh u-tee-lee-zey seht ohr-dee-naa-tuhr oh lyuh duh suh-lwee lah.

Do you know where I can buy discount computer parts?
Savez-vous où je peux acheter des pièces d'ordinateur en rabais ?
Saa-vey voo oo zhuh puh aa-shuh-tey dey pyehs dohr-dee-naa-tuhr ãn raa-beh ?

I have ten years of experience with Windows.
J'ai dix ans d'expérience avec Windows.
Zhey dee_zãn dehks-pey-ree-ãns aa-vehk ween-dohz.

What is the wi-fi password?
C'est quoi le mot de passe pour le wifi ?
Sey kwah luh moh duh pahs poor luh wee-fee ?

I need to have my login information reset.
J'ai besoin de réinitialiser mes informations de connexion.
Zhey buh-zwĩn duh rey-ee-nee-see-aa-lee-zey mey_zĩn-fohr-maa-syõn duh koh-nehk-syõn.

The hard drive is making a clicking noise.
Le disque dur fait un son de clic.
Luh deesk dur feh ũn sõn duh kleek.

How do I uninstall this program from my device?
Comment je fais pour désinstaller ce logiciel de mon appareil ?
Koh-mãn zhuh feh poor dey-zĩn-staa-ley suh loh-zhee-see-ehl duh mõn_naa-paa-rey-y ?

Can you help me set up a new account with this website?
Pouvez-vous m'aider à créer un nouveau compte sur ce site web ?
Poo-vey voo meh-dey aa krey-ey ũn noo-voh kõnt sur suh seet wehb ?

Why is the internet so slow?
Pourquoi l'internet est si lent ?
Poor-kwah lĩn-tehr-neht eh see lãn ?

Why is YouTube buffering every video I play?
Pourquoi YouTube tamponne chaque vidéo que je visionne ?
Poor-kwah yoo-toob tãm-pon shaak vee-dey-oh kuh zhuh vee-zee-on ?

My web camera isn't displaying a picture.
Ma webcam n'affiche aucune image.
Maa wehb-kaam naa-feesh oh-kun ee-maazh.

I have no bars on my phone.
Je n'ai aucune barre sur mon téléphone.
Zhuh ney oh-kun bahr sur mõn tey-ley-fon.

Where can I get my phone serviced?
Où puis-je faire réparer mon téléphone ?
Oo pweezh fehr rey-paa-rey mõn tey-ley-fon ?

My phone shows that it is charging but won't charge.
Mon téléphone affiche qu'il est en charge, mais il ne veut pas se charger.
Mõn tey-ley-fon aa-feesh keel eh_tãn shaarzh, meh eel nuh vuh pah suh shaar-zhey.

I think someone else is controlling my computer.
Je crois que quelqu'un d'autre contrôle mon ordinateur.
Zhuh krwah kuh kehl-kũn dohtr kõn-trohl mõn_nohr-dee-naa-tuhr.

My computer just gave a blue screen and shut down.
Mon ordinateur vient d'afficher l'écran bleu et de s'éteindre.
Mõn_nohr-dee-naa-tuhr vyĩn daa-fee-shey ley-krãn bluh ey duh sey-tĩndr.

Do you have the battery for this laptop?
Avez-vous la batterie pour cet ordinateur portable ?
Aa-vey voo laa baa-tree poor seht ohr-dee-naa-tuhr pohr-taabl.

Where can I get a compatible adapter?
Où pourrais-je obtenir un adaptateur compatible ?
Oo poo-rehzh ohb-tuh-neer ũn_naa-daap-taa-tuhr kõn-paa-teebl ?

I can't get online with the information you gave me.
Je ne peux pas me connecter à internet avec les informations que vous m'avez donné.
Zhuh nuh puh pah muh koh-nehk-tey aa ĩn-tehr-neht aa-vehk ley_zĩn-fohr-maa-syõn kuh voo maa-vey doh-ney.

This keyboard is not working correctly.
Le clavier ne fonctionne pas comme il faut.
Luh klaa-vee-ey nuh fõnk-syon pah kohm eel foh.

What is the login information for this computer?
Quelles sont les informations de connexion pour cet ordinateur ?
Kehl sõn ley_zĩn-fohr-maa-syõn duh koh-nehk-syõn poor seht ohr-dee-naa-tuhr ?

I need you to update my computer.
J'ai besoin que vous mettiez mon ordinateur à jour.
Zhey buh-zwĩn kuh voo meh-tyey mõn_nohr-dee-naa-tuhr aa zhoor.

Can you build my website?
Pouvez-vous me construire mon site web ?
Poo-vey voo muh kõn-stru-eer mõn seet wehb ?

I prefer Wordpress.
Je préfère Wordpress.
Zhuh prey-fehr wuhrd-prehs.

What are your rates per hour?
Quel est votre tarif horaire ?
Kehl eh vohtr taa-reef oh-rehr ?

Do you have experience handling email servers?
Avez-vous de l'expérience dans la gestion des serveurs de courriel ?
Aa-vey voo duh lehk-spey-ree-ãns dãn laa zhehs-tyõn dey sehr-vuhr duh koo-ree-ehl ?

I am locked out of my account, can you help?
Je suis bloqué de mon compte, pouvez-vous m'aider ?
Zhuh swee bloh-key duh mõn kõnt, poo-vey voo mey-dey ?

None of the emails I am sending are going through.
Aucun des courriels que j'envoie ne parvient à son destinataire.
Oh-kũn dey koo-ree-ehl kuh zhãn-vwah nuh paar-vyĩn aa sõn dehs-tee-naa-tehr.

96

The time and date on my computer are wrong.
L'heure et la date de mon ordinateur ne sont pas réglées.
Luhr ey laa daat duh mõn_nohr-dee-naa-tuhr nuh sõn pah rey-gley.

Is this game free to play?
C'est gratuit pour jouer à ce jeu ?
Sey graa-twee poor zhoo-ey aa suh zhuh ?

Where do I go to download the client?
Où dois-je aller pour télécharger le client ?
Oo dwahzh aa-ley poor tey-ley-shaar-zhey luh klee-ãn ?

I am having troubles chatting with my family.
J'ai des difficultés à chatter avec ma famille.
Zhey deh dee-fee-kul-tey aa chaa-tey aa-vehk maa faa-mee-y.

Is this the fastest computer here?
Est-ce que c'est l'ordinateur le plus rapide qu'il y a ici ?
Ehs-kuh sey lohr-dee-naa-tuhr luh plu raa-peed keel ee yah ee-see ?

How much space is on the computer?
L'ordinateur dispose de combien d'espace ?
Lohr-dee-naa-tuhr dees-pohz duh kõm-byĩn dehs-pahs ?

Will my profile be deleted once I log out? Or does it save?
Est-ce que mon profil sera supprimé lorsque je me déconnecte ? Ou il sera enregistré ?
Ehs-kuh mõn proh-feel suh-rah su-pree-mey lohr-skuh zhuh muh dey-koh-nehkt ? Oo eel suh-rah ãn-ruh-zhee-strey ?

How much do you charge for computer use?
Combien coûte l'utilisation des ordinateurs ?
Kõm-byĩn koot lu-tee-lee-zaa-syõn dey_zohr-dee-naa-tuhr ?

Are group discounts offered?
Offrez-vous des rabais de groupe ?
Oh-frey voo dey raa-beh duh groop ?

Can I use my own headphones with your computer?
Est-ce que je peux utiliser mes écouteurs avec votre ordinateur ?
Ehs-kuh zhuh puh u-tee-lee-zey mey_zey-koo-tuhr aa-vehk vohtr ohr-dee-naa-tuhr ?

Do you have a data cap?
Avez-vous un plafond de données ?
Aa-vey voo ũn plaa-fõn duh doh-ney ?

I think this computer has a virus.
Je crois que cet ordinateur a un virus.
Zhuh krwa kuh seht ohr-dee-naa-tuhr ah ũn vee-rus.

The battery for my laptop is running low.
La batterie de mon portable est presque à plat.
Laa baa-tree duh mõn pohr-taabl eh prehs_kaa plah.

Where can I plug this in? I need to recharge my device.
Où est-ce que je peux brancher ça ? Je dois charger mon appareil.
Oo ehs-kuh zhuh puh brãn-shey sah ? Zhuh dwah shaar-zhey mõn_naa-paa-reh-y.

Do you have a mini-USB cord?
Avez-vous un câble mini-USB ?
Aa-vey voo ũn kahbl mee-nee u-ehs-bey ?

Where can I go to watch the game?
Où puis-je aller pour voir le match ?
Oo pweezh aa-ley poor vwahr luh maach ?

Do you have an iPhone charger?
Avez-vous un chargeur pour iPhone ?
Aa-vey voo ũn shaar-zhuhr poor ee-fohn ?

I need a new battery for my watch.
Il me faut une nouvelle pile pour ma montre.
Eel muh foh un noo-vehl peel poor maa mõntr.

I need to borrow an HDMI cord.
J'ai besoin d'emprunter un fil HDMI.
Zhey buh-zwĩn dãm-prũn-tey ũn feel aash-dey-ehm-ee.

What happens when I exceed the data cap?
Qu'est-ce qui se passe lorsque je dépasse le plafond de données ?
Keh-skee suh pahs lohr-skuh zhuh dey-pahs luh plaa-fõn duh doh-ney ?

Can you help me pair my Bluetooth device ?
Pouvez-vous m'aider à coupler mon appareil Bluetooth ?
Poo-vey voo mey-dey aa koo-pley mõn_naa-paa-rey-y blu-tooth ?

I need a longer ethernet cord.
Il me faut un câble Ethernet plus long.
Eel muh foh ũn kahbl ey-tehr-neht plu lõn.

Why is this website restricted?
Pourquoi l'accès à ce site est limité ?
Poor-kwah laak-seh aa suh seet eh lee-mee-tey ?

How can I unblock this website?
Comment puis-je débloquer ce site web ?
Koh-mãn pweezh dey-bloh-key suh seet wehb ?

Is that television 4k or higher?
Cette télévision est 4k ou plus ?
Seht tey-ley-vee-zyõn eh kaatr kah oo plus ?

Do you have the Office suite on this computer?
Avez-vous la suite Office sur cet ordinateur ?
Aa-vey voo laa sweet oh-fees sur seht ohr-dee-naa-tuhr ?

This application won't install on my device.
L'application ne veut pas s'installer sur mon appareil.
Laa-plee-kaa-syõn nuh vuh pah sĩn-staa-ley sur mõn_naa-paa-rey-y.

Can you change the channel on the television?
Pouvez-vous changer la chaîne de télévision ?
Poo-vey voo shãn-zhey laa shehn duh tey-ley-vee-zyõn ?

I think a fuse blew.
Je crois qu'un fusible a sauté.
Zhuh krwah kũn fu-zeebl ah soh-tey.

The screen is black and won't come on.
L'écran est noir et ne veut pas s'allumer.
Ley-krãn eh nwahr ey nuh vuh pah saa-lu-mey.

I keep getting pop-ups on every website.
Je n'arrête pas d'avoir des pop-ups sur chaque site.
Zhuh naa-reht pah daa-vwahr dey poh-pohp sur shaak seet.

This computer is moving much slower than it should.
Cet ordinateur fonctionne beaucoup plus lentement qu'il devrait.
Seht ohr-dee-naa-tuhr fõnk-syon boh-koo plu lãnt-mãn keel duh-vreh.

I need to reactivate my copy of Windows.
Je dois réactiver ma copie de Windows.
Zhuh dwah rey-aak-tee-vey maa koh-pee duh ween-dohz.

Why is this website blocked on my laptop?
Pourquoi ce site est bloqué sur mon portable ?
Poor-kwah suh seet eh bloh-key sur mõn pohr-taabl ?

Can you show me how to download videos to my computer?
Pouvez-vous me montrer comment télécharger des vidéos sur mon ordinateur ?
Poo-vey voo muh mõn-trey koh-mãn tey-ley-shaar-zhey dey vee-dey-oh sur mõn ohr-dee-naa-tuhr ?

Can I insert a flash drive into this computer?
Est-ce que je peux insérer une clé USB dans cet ordinateur ?
Ehs-kuh zhuh puh ĩn-sey-rey un kley u-ehs-bey dãn seht ohr-dee-naa-tuhr ?

I want to change computers.
Je veux changer d'ordinateurs.
Zhuh vuh shãn-zhey dohr-dee-naa-tuhr.

Is Chrome the only browser I can use with this computer?
Chrome c'est le seul navigateur que je peux utiliser avec cet ordinateur ?
Krohm sey luh suhl naa-vee-gaa-tuhr kuh zhuh puh u-tee-lee-zey aa-vehk seht ohr-dee-naa-tuhr ?

Do you track my usage on any of these devices?
Est-ce que vous suivez mon utilisation sur ces appareils ?
Ehs-kuh voo swee-vey mõn u-tee-lee-zaa-syõn sur sey_zaa-paa-reh-y ?

CONVERSATION TIPS

Pardon me.
Pardonnez-moi.
Paar-doh-ney mwah.

Please speak more slowly.
S'il vous plaît parlez plus lentement.
Seel voo pleh paar-ley plu lãnt-mãn.

I don't understand.
Je ne comprends pas.
Zhuh nuh kõm-prãn pah.

Can you say that more clearly?
Pouvez-vous redire ça plus clairement ?
Poo-vey voo ruh-deer sah plu klehr-mãn ?

I don't speak Spanish very well.
Je ne parle pas bien l'espagnol.
Zhuh nuh paarl pah byĩn lehs-paa-nyohl.

Can you please translate that to English for me?
Pouvez-vous me traduire cela en anglais ?
Poo-vey voo muh traa-dweer suh-lah ãn_nãn-gleh ?

Let's talk over there where it is quieter.
Allons parler là-bas où il y a moins de bruit.
Aa-lõn paar-ley laa-bah oo eel ee ah mwĩn duh brwi.

Sit down over there.
Asseyez-vous là-bas.
Aa-sey-ey voo laa-bah.

May I?
Je peux ?
Zhuh puh ?

I am from America.
Je viens des États-Unis.
Zhuh vyĩn dey_zey-tah_zu-nee.

Am I talking too much?
Est-ce que je parle trop ?
Ehs-kuh zhuh paarl troh ?

I speak your language badly.
Je ne parle pas bien votre langue.
Zhuh nuh paarl pah byĩn vohtr lãn-g.

Am I saying that word correctly?
Est-ce que je dis ce mot correctement ?
Ehs-kuh zhuh dee suh moh koh-rehk-tuh-mãn ?

You speak English very well.
Vous parlez très bien l'anglais.
Voo paar-ley treh byĩn lãn-gleh.

This is my first time in your lovely country.
C'est ma première fois dans votre beau pays.
Sey maa pruh-myehr fwah dãn vohtr boh pey-ee.

Write that information down on this piece of paper.
Écrivez-moi cette information sur ce bout de papier.
Ey-kree-vey mwah seht ĩn-fohr-maa-syõn sur suh boo duh paa-pyey.

Do you understand?
Comprenez-vous ?
Kõm-pruh-ney voo ?

How do you pronounce that word?
Comment prononcez-vous ce mot ?
Koh-mãn proh-nõn-sey voo suh moh ?

Is this how you write this word?
C'est comme ça qu'on écrit ce mot ?
Sey kohm sah koh_ney-kree suh moh ?

Can you give me an example?

Pouvez-vous me donner un exemple ?

Poo-vey voo muh doh-ney ũn_neg-zãm-pl ?

Wait a moment, please.

Attendez un moment, s'il vous plaît.

Aa-tãn-dey ũn moh-mãn, seel voo pleh.

If there is anything you want, tell me.

Si vous voulez quelque chose, dites-le-moi.

See voo voo-ley kehl-kuh shohz, deet luh mwah.

I don't want to bother you anymore, so I will go.

Je ne veux pas vous déranger davantage donc je vais partir.

Zhuh nuh vuh pah voo dey-rãn-zhey daa-vãn-taazh dõnk zhuh veh paar-teer.

Please take care of yourself.

S'il vous plaît prenez-soin de vous-même.

Seel voo pleh pruh-ney swĩn duh voo-mehm.

When you arrive, let us know.

Informez-nous lorsque vous arrivez.

In-fohr-mey noo lohr-skuh voo_zaa-ree-vey.

DATE NIGHT

What is your telephone number?
Quel est votre numéro de téléphone ?
Kehl eh vohtr nu-mey-roh duh tey-ley-fon ?

I'll call you for the next date.
Je vous appellerais pour sortir encore.
Zhuh voo_zaa-pehl-uh-reh poor sohr-teer ãn-kahr.

I had a good time, can't wait to see you again.
Je me suis bien amusé, j'ai hâte de te revoir.
Zhuh muh swee byĩn_naa-mu-zey, zhey aht duh tuh ruh-vwahr.

I'll pay for dinner tonight.
Je vais payer pour dîner ce soir.
Zhuh veh pey-ey poor dee-neh suh swahr.

Dinner at my place?
On dîne chez moi ce soir ?
Õn deen shey mwah suh swahr ?

I don't think we should see each other anymore.
Je ne crois pas qu'on devrait continuer de se voir.
Zhuh nuh krwah pah kõn duh-vreh kõn-tee-nuey duh suh vwahr.

I'm afraid this will be the last time we see each other.
Je crains que c'est la dernière fois qu'on va se voir.
Zhuh krĩn kuh sey laa dehr-nyehr fwah kõn vah suh vwahr.

You look fantastic.
Tu es magnifique.
Tu eh maa-nyee-feek.

Would you like to dance with me?
Voulez-vous danser avec moi ?
Voo-ley voo dãn-sey aa-vehk mwah ?

Are there any 3D cinemas in this city?
Y-a-t-il des cinémas 3D dans cette ville ?
Ee-yah teel dey see-ney-mah trwah-dey dãn seht veel ?

We should walk along the beach.
On devrait se promener sur la plage.
Õn duh-vreh suh proh-muh-ney sur laa plaazh.

I hope you like my car.
J'espère que ma voiture vous plaît.
Zheh-spehr kuh maa vwah-tur voo pleh.

What movies are playing today?
Quels films sont en salle aujourd'hui ?
Kehl feelm sõn_tãn saal oh-zhoor-dwee ?

I've seen this film, but I wouldn't mind watching it again.
J'ai vu ce film, mais ça ne me dérangerait pas de le revoir.
Zhey vu suh feelm, meh saa nuh muh dey-rãn-zhuh-reh pah duh luh ruh-vwahr.

Do you know how to do the salsa?
Savez-vous danser la salsa ?
Saa-vey voo dãn-sey laa saal-sah ?

We can dance all night.
On peut danser toute la nuit.
Õn puh dãn-sey toot laa nwee.

I have some friends that will be joining us tonight.
J'ai quelques amis qui vont nous rejoindre ce soir.
Zhey kehl-kuh_zaa-mee kee võn noo ruh-zhwĩndr suh swahr.

Is this a musical or a regular concert?
C'est une comédie musicale ou un concert normal ?
Sey_tun koh-mey-dee mu-zee-kaal oo ũn kõn-sehr nohr-maal ?

Did you get VIP tickets?
Vous avez eu des billets VIP ?
Voo_zaa-vey u dey bee-eh vey-ee-pey ?

I'm going to have to cancel on you tonight. Maybe another time?
Je dois annuler pour ce soir. Peut-être qu'on peut le reporter ?
Zhuh dwah aa-nu-ley suh swahr. Puh_teh-tr kõn puh luh ruh-pohr-tey ?

If you want, we can go to your place.
Si tu veux, on peut aller chez toi.
See tu vuh, õn puh aa-ley shey twah.

I'll pick you up tonight.
Je viendrais te chercher ce soir.
Zhuh vyĩn-dreh tuh shehr-shey suh swahr.

This one is for you!
Celle-là est pour toi !
Sehl-lah eh poor twah !

What time does the party start?
À quelle heure la fête commence ?
Aa kehl uhr laa feht koh-mãns ?

Will it end on time or will you have to leave early?
Ça va se terminer à l'heure, ou tu vas devoir quitter tôt ?
Saa vah suh tehr-mee-ney aa luhr, oo tu vah duh-vwahr kee-tey toh ?

Did you like your gift?
Tu as aimé ton cadeau ?
Tu ah eh-mey tõn kaa-doh ?

I want to invite you to watch a movie with me tonight.
J'aimerais vous inviter à voir un film avec moi ce soir.
Zheh-muh-reh voo_zĩn-vee-tey aa vwahr ũn feelm aa-vehk mwah suh swahr.

Do you want anything to drink?
Voulez-vous quelque chose à boire ?
Voo-ley voo kehl-kuh shohz aa bwahr ?

I am twenty-six years old.
J'ai vingt-six ans.
Zhey vĩn_tsee_zãn.

You're invited to a small party I'm having at my house.
Vous êtes invité à une petite fête chez moi.
Voo_zeht ĩn-vee-tey aa un puh-teet feht shey mwah.

I love you.
Je t'aime.
Zhuh tehm.

We should go to the arcade.
On devrait aller à la salle de jeux.
Õn duh-vreh aa-ley aa laa saal duh zhuh.

Have you ever played this game before?
Avez-vous joué à ce jeu auparavant ?
Aa-vey voo zhoo-ey aa suh zhuh oh-paa-raa-vãn ?

Going on this ferry would be really romantic.
Ça serait très romantique de prendre ce ferry.
Saa suh-reh treh roh-mãn-teek duh prãndr suh fey-ree.

How about a candlelight dinner?
Qu'en-dis-tu d'un dîner aux chandelles ?
Kãn-dee-tu dũn dee-ney oh shãn-dehl ?

Let's dance and sing!
Dansons et chantons !
Dãn-sõn ey shãn-tõn !

Will you marry me?
Veux-tu m'épouser ?
Vuh-tu mey-poo-zey ?

Set the table, please.
Mettez la table, s'il vous plaît.
Meh-tey laa taabl, seel voo pleh.

Here are the dishes and the glasses.
Voici les assiettes et les verres.
Vwah-see ley_zaa-syeht ey ley vehr.

Where is the cutlery?
Où sont les couverts ?
Oo sõn ley koo-vehr ?

May I hold your hand?
Est-ce que je peux te prendre la main ?
Ehs-kuh zhuh puh tuh prãndr laa mĩn ?

Let me get that for you.
Laissez-moi vous aider.
Leh-sey mwah voo_zeh-dey.

I think our song is playing!
C'est notre chanson qui joue !
Sey nohtr shãn-sõn kee zhoo !

Let's make a wish together.
Faisons un vœu ensemble.
Feh-zõn ũn vuh ãn-sãmbl.

Is there anything that you want from me?
Tu veux quelque chose de ma part ?
Tu vuh kehl-kuh shohz duh maa pahr ?

There is nowhere I would rather be than right here with you.
Il n'y a nulle part je préférerais être qu'ici avec toi.
Eel nee ah nul pahr zhuh prey-feh-ruh-reh ehtr kee-see aa-vehk twah.

I'll give you a ride back to your place.
Je te donnerais un lift pour retourner chez toi.
Zhuh tuh doh-nuh-reh ũn leeft poor ruh-toor-ney shey twah.

Would you like me to hold your purse?
Tu veux que je te tienne ton sac ?
Tu vuh kuh zhuh tuh tyehn tõn saak ?

Let's pray before we eat our meal.
Prions avant de manger notre repas.
Pree-yõn aa-vãn duh mãn-zhey nohtr ruh-pah.

Do you need a napkin?
Avez-vous besoin d'une serviette ?
Aa-vey voo buh-zwĩn dun sehr-vee-eht ?

I'm thirsty.
J'ai soif.
Zhey swahf.

I hope you enjoy your meal.
J'espère que vous aurez un bon repas.
Zheh-spehr kuh voo_zoh-rey ũn bõn ruh-pah.

I need to add more salt to the salt shaker.
Je dois remplir la salière.
Zhuh dwah rãm-pleer laa saa-lyehr.

We should get married!
On devrait se marier !
Õn duh-vreh suh maa-ree-ey !

How old are you?
Quel âge avez-vous ?
Kehl ahzh aa-vey voo ?

Will you dream of me?
Tu vas rêver de moi ?
Tu vah reh-vey duh mwah ?

Thank you very much for the wonderful date last night.
Merci beaucoup pour la sortie merveilleuse hier soir.
Mehr-see boh-koo poor laa sohr-tee mehr-veh-yuhz ee-ehr swahr.

Would you like to come to a party this weekend?
Aimeriez-vous venir à une fête ce week-end ?
Eh-muh-ree-ey voo vuh-neer aa un feht suh week-ehnd ?

This Saturday night, right?
Ce samedi soir, c'est ça ?
Suh sehm-dee swahr, sey sah ?

I will be lonely without you.
Je vais me sentir seul sans toi.
Zhuh veh muh sãn-teer suhl sãn twah.

Please stay the night?
S'il te plaît reste pour la nuit ?
Seel tuh pleh rehst poor laa nwee ?

I like your fragrance.
J'aime votre parfum.
Zhehm vohtre paar-fũm.

That is a beautiful outfit you're wearing.
C'est une très belle tenue que vous portez.
Sey_tun treh behl tuh-nu kuh voo pohr-tey.

You look beautiful.
Tu es très belle.
Tu eh treh behl.

Let me help you out of the car.
Laissez-moi vous aider à sortir de la voiture.
Leh-sey mwah voo_zeh-dey aa sohr-teer duh laa vwah-tur.

Sarah, will you come with me to dinner?
Sarah, viendrais-tu dîner avec moi ?
Saa-rah, vyîn-dreh tu dee-ney aa-vehk mwah ?

I would like to ask you out on a date.
J'aimerais vous demander de sortir avec moi.
Zheh-muh-reh voo duh-mãn-dey duh sohr-teer aa-vehk mwah.

Are you free tonight?
Êtes-vous libre ce soir ?
Eht voo leebr suh swahr ?

This is my phone number. Call me anytime.
Voici mon numéro de téléphone. Appelez-moi n'importe quand.
Vwah-see mõn nu-mey-roh duh tey-ley-fon. Aa-puh-lez mwah nĩm-port kãn.

Can I hug you?
Je peux vous faire un câlin ?
Zhuh puh voo fehr ŭn kaa-lĭn ?

Would you like to sing karaoke?
Aimeriez-vous faire du karaoké ?
Eh-muh-rey voo fehr du kaa-raa-oh-key ?

What kind of song would you like to sing?
Quel genre de chanson voulez-vous chanter ?
Kehl zhãnr duh shãn-sõn voo-ley voo shãn-tey ?

Have you ever sung this song before?
Avez-vous chanté cette chanson avant ?
Aa-vey voo shãn-tey seht shãn-sõn aa-vãn ?

We can sing it together.
On peut la chanter ensemble.
Õn puh laa shãn-tey ãn-sãmbl.

Can I kiss you?
Je peux t'embrasser ?
Zhuh puh tãm-braa-sey ?

Are you cold?
Avez-vous froid ?
Aa-vey voo frwah ?

We can stay out as late as you want.
On peut rester jusqu'à l'heure que tu veux.
Õn puh rehs-tey zhus-kaa luhr kuh tu vuh.

Please, dinner is on me.
S'il te plaît, c'est moi qui t'invite. Je vais payer.
Seel tuh pleh, sey mwah kee tĭn-veet. Zhuh veh pey-ey.

Shall we split the bill?
On partage l'addition ?
Õn paar-taazh laa-dee-syõn ?

We should spend more time together.
On devrait passer plus de temps ensemble.
Õn duh-vreh pah-sey plus duh tãn ãn-sãmbl.

We should walk the town tonight.
On devrait se promener dans la ville ce soir.
Õn duh-vreh suh proh-muh-ney dãn laa veel suh swahr

Did you enjoy everything?
Tout vous a plu ?
Too voo_zah plu ?

MONEY AND SHOPPING

May I try this on?
Je peux essayer cela ?
Zhuh puh eh-sey-ey suh-lah ?

How much does this cost?
Combien ça coûte ça ?
Kõm-byĩn saa koot sah ?

Do I sign here or here?
Je signe ici ou ici ?
Zhuh seen-y ee-see oo ee-see ?

Is that your final price?
C'est votre prix final ?
Sey vohtr pree fee-naal ?

Where do I find toiletries?
Où pourrais-je trouver les produits de toilette ?
Oo poo-rehzh troo-vey ley proh-dwee duh twah-leht ?

Would you be willing to take five dollars for this item?
Cinq dollars pour cet article, ça vous irait ?
Sĩnk doh-lahr poor seht aar-teekl, saa voo_zee-reh ?

I can't afford it at that price.
Je peux pas me le permettre à ce prix.
Zhuh puh pah muh luh pehr-mehtr aa suh pree.

I can find this cheaper somewhere else.
Ça je peux le trouver moins cher ailleurs.
Sah zhuh puh luh troo-vey mwĩn shehr ah-yuhr.

Is there a way we can haggle on price?
On peut négocier le prix ?
Õn puh ney-goh-see-ey luh pree ?

How many of these have sold today?
Combien vous avez vendu de ça aujourd'hui ?
Kõm-byĩn voo_zaa-vey vãn-du duh sah oh-zhoor-dwee ?

Can you wrap that up as a gift?
Pouvez-vous emballer ça en cadeau ?
Poo-vey voo ãm-baa-ley sah ãn kaa-doh ?

Do you provide personalized letters?
Faites-vous les lettres personnalisées ?
Feht voo ley lehtr pehr-soh-naa-lee-zey ?

I would like this to be special delivered to my hotel.
J'aimerais qu'on me livre ça à mon hôtel.
Zheh-muh-reh kõn muh leevr sah aa mõn_noh-tehl.

Can you help me, please?
Pouvez-vous m'aider, s'il vous plaît ?
Poo-vey voo mey-dey, seel voo pleh ?

We should go shopping at the market.
On devrait aller faire du shopping au marché.
Õn duh-vreh aa-ley fehr du shoh-peeng oh maar-shey.

Are you keeping track of the clothes that fit me?
Tu notes les vêtements qui sont de ma taille ?
Tu noht ley veht-mãn kee sõn duh maa tah-y ?

Can I have one size up?
Je peux avoir la prochaine taille plus grande ?
Zhuh puh aa-vwahr laa proh-shehn tah-y plu grãnd ?

How many bathrooms does the apartment have?
Combien il y a de salles de bain dans l'appartement ?
Kõm-byĩn eel ee yah duh saal duh bĩn dãn laa-paar-tuh-mãn ?

Where's the kitchen?
Où se trouve la cuisine ?
Oo suh troov laa kwee-zeen ?

Does this apartment have a gas or electric stove?
Cet appartement a une cuisinière au gaz ou à l'électricité ?
Seht aa-paar-tuh-mãn aa un kwee-zee-nyehr oh gahz oo aa ley-lehk-tree-see-tey ?

Is there a spacious backyard?
Il y a une grande arrière-cour ?
Eel ee yah un grãnd aa-ryehr coor ?

How much is the down payment?
C'est combien l'acompte ?
Sey kõm-byĩn laa-kõnt ?

I'm looking for a furnished apartment.
Je cherche un appartement meublé.
Zhuh shehr-sh ũn_naa-paar-tuh-mãn muh-bley.

I need a two-bedroom apartment to rent.
J'ai besoin d'un appartement F3 à louer.
Zhey buh-zwĩn dũn_naa-paar-tuh-mãn ehf-trwah aa loo-ey.

I'm looking for an apartment with utilities paid.
Je cherche un appartement avec services inclus.
Zhuh shehr-sh ũn_naa-paar-tuh-mãn aa-vehk sehr-veez ĩn-klu.

The carpet in this apartment needs to be pulled up.
Le tapis dans cet appartement doit être enlevé.
Luh taa-pee dãn seht aa-paar-tuh-mãn dwah_tehtr ãn-luh-vey.

I need you to come down on the price of this apartment.
J'ai besoin que vous baissiez le prix de cet appartement.
Zhey buh-zwĩn kuh voo beh-syey luh pree duh seht aa-paar-tuh-mãn.

Will I be sharing this place with other people?
Je partagerais cette espace avec d'autres gens ?
Zhuh paar-taa-zhuh-reh seht ehs-pahs aa-vehk dohtr zhãn ?

How do you work the fireplace?
Comment le foyer fonctionne-t-il ?
Koh-mãn luh fwah-yey fõnk-syon-teel ?

Are there any curfew rules attached to this apartment?
Y-a-t-il des règles de couvre-feu dans cet appartement ?
Ee-ya teel dey rehgl duh koov-ruh-fuh dãn seht aa-paar-tuh-mãn ?

How long is the lease for this place?
C'est quoi la durée du bail pour ce lieu ?
Sey kwah laa du-rey du bah-y poor suh lyuh ?

Do you gamble?
Vous aimez les jeux de pari ?
Voo_zeh-mey ley zhuh duh paa-ree ?

We should go to a casino.
On devrait aller à un casino.
Õn duh-vreh aa-ley aa ũn kaa-zee-noh.

There is really good horse racing in this area.
Il y a des bonnes courses de chevaux dans cette région.
Eel ee yah dey bon koors duh shuh-voh dãn seht rey-zhee-õn.

Do you have your ID so that we can go gambling?
Avez-vous votre pièce d'identité pour qu'on puisse aller jouer ?
Aa-vey voo vohtr pyehs dee-dãn-tee-tey poor kõn pwees aa-ley zhoo-ey ?

Who did you bet on?
Sur qui vous avez parié ?
Sur kee voo_zaa-vey paa-ree-ey ?

I am calling about the apartment that you placed in the ad.
Je vous appelle au sujet de l'appartement que vous avez mis dans l'annonce.
Zhuh voo_zaa-pehl oh su-zheh duh laa-paar-tuh-mãn kuh voo_zaa-vey mee dãn laa-nõns.

How much did you bet?
Combien vous avez parié ?
Kõm-byĩn voo_zaa-vey paa-ree-ey ?

We should go running with the bulls!
On devrait aller faire la course avec les taureaux !
Õn duh-vreh aa-ley fehr laa koors aa-vehk ley toh-roh !

Is Adele coming to sing at this venue tonight?
Est-ce qu'Adèle vient chanter ici ce soir ?
Ehs-kaa-dehl vyĩn shãn-tey ee-see suh swahr ?

How much is the item you have in the window?
Combien coûte l'article dans votre fenêtre ?
Kõm-byĩn koot laar-teekl dãn vohtr fuh-nehtr ?

Do you have payment plans?
Avez-vous des plans de paiement ?
Aa-vey voo dey plãn duh pey-mãn ?

Do these two items come together?
Ces deux articles viennent ensemble ?
Sey duh_zaar-teekl vyehn ãn-sãmbl ?

Are these parts cheaply made?
Ces pièces sont fabriquées à bas coût ?
Sey pyehs sõn faa-bree-key aa bah koo ?

This is a huge bargain!
C'est une très bonne affaire !
Sey-tun treh bo_naa-fehr !

I like this. How does three hundred dollars sound?
J'aime bien ça. Qu'en diriez-vous de trois cent dollars ?
Zhehm byĩn sah. Kãn dee-ree-ey voo duh trwah sãn doh-lahr ?

Two hundred is all I can offer. That is my final price.
Je peux pas offrir plus de deux cent. C'est mon prix final.
Zhuh puh pah oh-freer plus duh duh sãn. Sey mõn pree fee-naal.

Do you have cheaper versions of this item?
Avez-vous des versions moins chères de cet article ?
Aa-vey voo dey vehr-zyõn mwĩn shehr duh seht aar-teekl ?

Do you have the same item with a different pattern?
Avez-vous le même article avec un autre motif ?
Aa-vey voo luh mehm aar-teekl aa-vehk ũn_nohtr moh-teef ?

How much is this worth?
Ça vaut combien ça ?
Saa voh kõm-byĩn sah ?

Can you pack this up and send it to my address on file?
Pouvez-vous emballer ceci et l'envoyer à mon adresse que vous avez au dossier ?
Poo-vey voo ãm-baa-ley suh-see ey lãn-vwah-yey aa mõn_naa-drehs kuh voo_zaa-vey oh doh-see-ey ?

Does it fit?
Ça rentre ?
Saa rãntr ?

They are too big for me.
Ils sont trop grands pour moi.
Eel sõn troh grãn poor mwah.

Please find me another but in the same size.
S'il vous plaît trouvez-moi une autre mais de la même taille.
Seel voo pleh troo-vey mwah un_nohtr meh duh laa mehm tah-y.

It fits, but is tight around my waist.
Ça me va, mais c'est serré autour de ma taille.
Saa muh vah, meh sey sey-rey oh-toor duh maa tah-y.

Can I have one size down?
Je peux avoir la prochaine taille plus petite ?
Zhuh puh aa-vwahr laa proh-shehn tah-y plu puh-teet ?

Size twenty, American.
Taille vingt en taille américaine.
Tah-y vĩn ãn tah-y aa-mey-ree-kehn.

Do you sell appliances for the home?
Vendez-vous des appareils électroménagers ?
Vãn-dey voo dey_zaa-paa-reh-y ey-lehk-troh-mey-naa-zhey ?

Not now, thank you.
Pas maintenant, merci.
Pah mĩn-tuh-nãn, mehr-see.

I'm looking for something special.
Je cherche quelque chose de spécial.
Zhuh shehr-sh kehl-kuh shohz duh spey-see-aal.

I'll call you when I need you.
Je vous appelerais lorsque j'aurais besoin de vous.
Zhuh voo_zaa-peh-luh-reh lohr-skuh zhoh-reh buh-zwĩn duh voo.

Do you have this in my size?
Avez-vous ceci dans ma taille ?
Aa-vey voo suh-see dãn maa tah-y ?

On which floor can I find cologne?
À quel étage je trouverais l'eau de Cologne ?
Aa kehl ey-taazh zhuh troo-vuh-reh loh duh koh-loh-ny ?

Where is the entrance?
Où se trouve l'entrée ?
Oo suh troov lãn-trey ?

Do I exit from that door?
Je peux sortir par cette porte ?
Zhuh puh sohr-teer paar seht pohrt ?

Where is the elevator?
Où se trouve l'ascenseur ?
Oo suh troov laa-sãn-suhr ?

Do I push or pull to get this door open?
Je dois pousser ou tirer cette porte pour l'ouvrir ?
Zhuh dwah poo-sey oo tee-rey seht pohrt poor loo-vreer ?

I already have that, thanks.
Je l'ai déjà, merci.
Zhuh ley dey-zhah, mehr-see.

Where can I try this on?
Où est-ce que je peux essayer cela ?
Oo ehs-kuh zhuh puh eh-sey-ey suh-lah ?

This mattress is very soft.
Ce matelas est très doux.
Suh maat-lah eh treh doo.

What is a good place for birthday gifts?
C'est quoi un bon coin pour les cadeaux d'anniversaire ?
Sey kwah ũn bõn kwĩn poor ley kaa-doh daa-nee-vehr-sehr ?

I'm just looking, but thank you.
Je fais juste regarder, mais merci.
Zhuh feh zhust ruh-gaar-dey, meh mehr-see.

Yes, I will call you when I need you, thank you.
Oui, je vous appelerais lorsque j'aurais besoin de vous, merci.
Wee, zhuh voo_zaa-peh-luh-reh lohr-skuh zhoh-reh buh-zwĩn duh voo, mehr-see.

Do you accept returns?
Vous acceptez les retours ?
Voo_zaak-sehp-tey ley ruh-toor ?

Here is my card and receipt for the return.
Voici ma carte et mon reçu pour le retour.
Vwah-see maa kaart ey mõn ruh-su poor luh ruh-toor.

Where are the ladies' clothes?
Où sont les vêtements pour femme ?
Oo sõn ley veht-mãn poor faam ?

What sizes are available for this item?
Quelles tailles sont disponibles pour cet article ?
Kehl tah-y sõn dees-poh-neebl poor seht aar-teekl ?

Is there an ATM machine nearby?
Y-a-t-il un guichet automatique dans le coin ?
Ee-yah teel ũn gee-sheh oh-toh-maa-teek dãn luh kwĩn ?

What forms of payment do you accept?
Quelles modes de paiement acceptez-vous ?
Kehl mohd duh pey-mãn aak-sehp-tey voo ?

That doesn't interest me.
Ça ne m'intéresse pas.
Saa nuh mĩn-tey-rehs pah.

I don't like it, but thank you.
Ça me plaît pas, mais merci.
Saam pleh pah, meh mehr-see.

Do you take American dollars?
Vous acceptez les dollars américains ?
Voo_zaak-sehp-tey ley doh-lahr aa-mey-ree-kĩn ?

Can you make change for me ?
Vous pouvez me faire de la monnaie ?
Voo poo-vey muh fehr duh laa moh-neh ?

What is the closest place to get change for my money ?
C'est quoi le coin le plus proche que je pourrais changer mes billets en monnaie ?
Sey kwah luh kwĩn luh plu prohsh kuh zhuh poo-reh shãn-zhey mey bee-eh ãn moh-neh ?

Are travelers checks able to be changed here?
C'est possible d'échanger les chèques de voyage ici ?
Sey poh-seebl dey-shãnzhey ley shehk duh vwah-yaazh ee-see ?

What is the current exchange rate?
Quel est le taux de change actuel ?
Kehl eh luh toh duh shãnzh aak-tu-ehl ?

What is the closest place to exchange money?
Quel est le coin le plus proche qu'on peut échanger de l'argent ?
Kehl eh luh kwĩn luh plu prohsh kõn puh ey-shãn-zhey duh laar-zhãn ?

Do you need to borrow money? How much?
Vous avez besoin d'emprunter de l'argent ? Combien ?
Voo_zaa-vey buh-zwĩn dãn-prũn-tey duh laar-zhãn ? Kõm-byĩn ?

Can this bank exchange my money?
Est-ce que cette banque peut échanger mon argent ?
Ehs-kuh seht bãnk puh ey-shãn-zhey mõn_naar-zhãn ?

121

What is the exchange rate for the American dollar?
C'est quoi le taux de change pour le dollar américain ?
Sey kwah luh toh duh shãnzh poor luh doh-lahr aa-mey-ree-kĩn ?

Will you please exchange me fifty dollars?
Pourriez-vous m'échanger cinquante dollars ?
Poo-ree-ey voo mey-shãn-zhey sĩn-kãnt doh-lahr ?

I would like a receipt with that.
J'aimerais avoir un reçu, s'il vous plaît.
Zheh-muh-reh aa-vwahr ũn ruh-su, seel voo pleh.

Your commission rate is too high.
Votre taux de commission est trop élevé.
Vohtr toh duh koh-mee-syõn eh troh_zey-luh-vey.

Does this bank have a lower commission rate?
Est-ce que cette banque a un taux de commission moins élevé ?
Ehs-kuh seht bãnk ah ũn toh duh koh-mee-syõn mwĩn_ zey-luh-vey

Do you take cash?
Vous acceptez les espèces ?
Voo_zaak-sehp-tey ley_zehs-pehs ?

Where can I exchange dollars?
Où est-ce que je pourrais échanger des dollars ?
Oo ehs-kuh zhuh poo-reh ey-shãn-zhey dey doh-lahr ?

I want to exchange dollars for yen.
Je veux échanger des dollars pour des yens.
Zhuh vuh ey-shãn-zhey dey doh-lahr poor dey yehn.

Do you take credit cards?
Vous prenez les cartes de crédit ?
Voo pruh-ney ley kaart duh krey-dee ?

Here is my credit card.
Voici ma carte de crédit.
Vwah-see maa kaart duh krey-dee.

One moment, let me check the receipt.
Un instant, laissez-moi vérifier le reçu.
Un_nĩn-stãn, leh-sey mwah vey-ree-fee-ey luh ruh-su.

Do I need to pay tax?
Est-ce que je dois payer une taxe ?
Ehs-kuh zhuh dwah pey-ey un taaks ?

How much is this item with tax?
Combien ça coûte ça avec taxe ?
Kõm-byĩn saa koot sah aa-vehk taaks ?

Where is the cashier?
Où est le caissier ?
Oo eh luh key-see-ey ?

Excuse me, I'm looking for a dress.
Pardonnez-moi, je cherche une robe.
Paar-doh-ney mwah, zhuh shehr-sh un rohb.

That's a lot for that dress.
C'est cher pour cette robe.
Sey shehr poor seht rohb.

Sorry, but I don't want it.
Désolée, mais je ne le veux pas.
Dey-zoh-ley, meh zhuh nuh luh vuh pah.

Okay I will take it.
D'accord, je le prendrais.
Daa-kohr, zhuh luh prãn-dreh.

I'm not interested if you are going to sell it at that price.
Ça ne m'intéresse pas si vous allez le vendre à ce prix.
Saa nuh mĩn-tey-rehs pah see voo_zaa-ley luh vãndr aa suh pree.

You are cheating me at the current price.
Vous m'arnaquez à ce prix.
Voo maar-naa-key aa suh pree.

No thanks. I'll only take it if you lower the price by half.
Non merci. Je le prendrais seulement si vous diminuez le prix de 50%.
Nõn mehr-see. Zhuh luh prãn-dreh suhl-mãn see voo dee-mee-nu-ey luh pree duh sĩn-kãnt poor-sãn.

That is a good price, I'll take it.
C'est un bon prix, je le prendrais.
Sey_tũn bõn pree, zhuh luh prãn-dreh.

Do you sell souvenirs for tourists?
Vendez-vous des souvenirs pour touristes ?
Vãn-dey voo dey soo-vneer poor too-reest ?

Can I have a bag for that?
Je peux avoir un sac pour ça ?
Zhuh puh aa-vwahr ũn saak poor sah ?

Is this the best bookstore in the city?
Est-ce que c'est la meilleure librairie dans la ville ?
Ehs-kuh sey laa meh-yuhr lee-breh-ree dãn laa veel ?

I would like to go to a game shop to buy comic books.
J'aimerais aller à un magasin de jeux pour acheter des bandes dessinées.
Zheh-muh-reh aa-ley aa ũn maa-gaa-zĩn duh zhuh poor aa-shuh-tey dey bãnd dey-see-ney.

Are you able to ship my products overseas?
Êtes-vous capable d'expédier mes produits à l'étranger ?
Eht voo kaa-paabl dehks-pey-dee-ey mey proh-dwee aa ley-trãn-zhey ?

CHILDREN AND PETS

Which classroom does my child attend?
Dans quelle salle de classe mon enfant assiste ?
Dãn kehl saal duh klahs mõn_nãn-fãn aa-seest ?

Is the report due before the weekend?
Le rapport doit être soumis avant le week-end ?
Luh raa-pohr dwah_tehtr soo-mee aa-vãn luh wee-kehnd ?

I'm waiting for my mom to pick me up.
J'attends ma mère qui vient me chercher.
Zhaa-tãn maa mehr kee vyĩn muh shehr-shey.

What time does the school bus run?
À quelle heure l'autobus marche ?
Aa kehl uhr loh-toh-bus maarsh ?

I need to see the principal.
J'ai besoin de voir le directeur.
Zhey buh-zwĩn duh vwahr luh dee-rehk-tuhr.

I would like to report bullying.
J'aimerais signaler de l'intimidation.
Zheh-muh-reh see-nyaa-ley duh lĩn-tee-mee-daa-syõn.

What are the leash laws in this area?
Quelles sont les lois sur les laisses dans cette région ?
Kehl sõn ley lwah sur ley lehs dãn seht rey-zhyõn ?

Please keep your dog away from mine.
S'il vous plaît gardez votre chien loin du mien.
Seel voo pleh gaar-dey vohtr shyĩn lwĩn du myĩn.

My dog doesn't bite.
Mon chien ne mord pas.
Mõn shyĩn nuh mohr pah.

I am allergic to cat hair.
Je suis allergique aux poils de chat.
Zhuh swee_zaa-lehr-zheek oh pwahl duh shah.

Don't leave the door open or the cat will run out!
Ne laissez pas la porte ouverte, si non le chat va fuir !
Nuh leh-sey pah laa pohrt oo-vehrt, see nõn luh shah vah fweer !

Have you fed the dogs yet?
As-tu fait manger le chien ou pas encore ?
Ah tu feh mãn-zhey luh shyĩn oo pah_zãn-kahr ?

We need to take the dog to the veterinarian.
On doit prendre le chien au vétérinaire.
Õn dwah prãndr luh shyĩn oh vey-tey-ree-nehr.

Are there any open roster spots on the team?
Y-a-t-il des places ouvertes sur l'équipe ?
Ee-yah teel dey plaas oo-vehrt sur ley-keep ?

My dog is depressed.
Mon chien est déprimé.
Mõn shyĩn eh dey-pree-mey.

Don't feed the dog table scraps.
Ne donnez pas les restes de table au chien.
Nuh doh-ney pah ley rehst duh taabl oh shyĩn.

Don't let the cat climb up on the furniture.
Ne laisse pas le chat grimper sur les meubles.
Nuh lehs pah luh shah grĩm-pey sur ley muhbl.

The dog is not allowed to sleep in the bed with you.
Le chien n'a pas le droit de dormir avec toi dans le lit.
Luh shyĩn nah pah luh drwah duh dohr-meer aa-vehk twah dãn luh lee.

There is dog poop on the floor. Clean it up.
Il y a des crottes de chien par terre. Nettoie-les.
Eel ee yah dey krot duh shyĩn paar tehr. Neh-twah ley.

When was the last time you took the dog for a walk?
C'est quand la dernière fois que tu as promené le chien ?
Sey kãn laa dehr-nyehr fwah kuh tu ah proh-muh-ney luh shyĩn ?

Are you an international student? How long are you attending?
Vous êtes un étudiant étranger ? Pour combien de temps vous assistez ?
Voo_zeht ũn_ney-tu-dyãn ey-trãn-zhey ? Poor kõm-byĩn duh tãn voo_zaa-see-stey ?

Are you a French student?
Vous êtes un étudiant français ?
Voo_zeht ũn_ney-tu-dyãn frãn-seh ?

I am an American student that is here for the semester.
Je suis un étudiant américain, je suis là pour le semestre.
Zhuh swee_zũn_ney-tu-dyãn aa-mey-ree-kĩn, zhuh swee lah poor luh suh-mehstr.

Please memorize this information.
S'il vous plaît mémorisez ces informations.
Seel voo pleh mey-moh-ree-zey sey_zĩn-fohr-maa-syõn.

This is my roommate Max.
Voici mon coloc Max.
Vwah-see mõn koh-lok Maaks.

Are these questions likely to appear on the exams?
Ces questions vont probablement apparaître dans les examens ?
Sey kehs-tyõn võn proh-baa-bluh-mãn aa-paa-rehtr dãn ley_zehg-zaa-mĩn ?

Teacher, say that once more, please.
Prof, vous pouvez répéter ça encore une fois, s'il vous plaît ?
Prohf, voo poo-vey rey-pey-tey sah ãn-kahr un fwah, seel voo pleh ?

I didn't do well on the quiz.
Je n'ai pas eu un bon résultat dans le quiz.
Zhuh ney pah u ũn bõn rey-zul-tah dãn luh kweez.

Go play outside, but stay where I can see you.
Va jouer dehors, mais reste où je peux te voir.
Vah zhoo-ey duh-ohr, meh rehst oo zhuh puh tuh vwahr.

How is your daughter?
Comment va votre fille ?
Koh-mãn vah vohtr fee-y ?

I'm going to walk the dogs.
Je vais aller promener les chiens.
Zhuh veh aa-ley proh-muh-ney ley shyĩn.

She's not very happy here.
Elle n'est pas très heureuse ici.
Ehl neh pah treh_zuh-ruhz ee-see.

I passed the quiz with high marks!
J'ai eu des bonnes marques dans le quiz !
Zhey u dey bon maark dãn luh kweez !

What program are you enrolled in?
Vous êtes inscrit dans quel programme ?
Voo_zeht ĩn-skree dãn kehl proh-graam ?

I really like my English teacher.
J'aime beaucoup mon professeur d'anglais.
Zhehm boh-koo mõn proh-feh-suhr dãn-gleh.

I have too much homework to do.
J'ai trop de devoirs à faire.
Zhey troh duh duh-vwahr aa fehr.

Tomorrow, I have to take my dog to the vet.
Demain, je dois prendre mon chien au vétérinaire.
Duh-mĩn, zhuh dwah prãndr mõn shyĩn oh vey-tey-ree-nehr.

When do we get to go to lunch?
À quelle heure on peut aller déjeuner ?
Aa kehl uhr õn puh aa-ley dey-zhuh-ney ?

My dog swallowed something he shouldn't have.
Mon chien a avalé quelque chose qu'il n'aurait pas du.
Mõn shyĩn ah aa-vaa-ley kehl-kuh shohz keel noh-reh pah du.

We need more toys for our dog to play with.
On a besoin de plus de jouets pour notre chien.
Õn_nah buh-zwĩn duh plus duh zhoo-eh poor nohtr shyĩn.

Can you please change the litter box?
Peux-tu nettoyer le bac à litière ?
Puh tu neh-twah-yey luh baak aa lee-tyehr ?

Get a lint brush and roll it to get the hair off your clothes.
Va chercher une brosse à charpie et enlève les poils de tes vêtements.
Vah shehr-shey un brohs aa shaar-pee ey ãn-lehv ley pwahl duh tey veht-mãn.

Can you help me study?
Pouvez-vous m'aider à étudier ?
Poo-vey voo mey-dey aa ey-tu-dyey ?

I have to go study in my room.
Je dois aller étudier dans ma chambre.
Zhuh dwah aa-ley ey-tu-dyey dãn maa shãmbr.

We went to the campus party, and it was a lot of fun.
On a assisté à la fête sur campus, et c'était vraiment sympa.
Õn_nah aa-see-stey aa laa feht sur kãm-pus, ey sey-tey vreh-mãn sĩm-paa.

Can you use that word in a sentence?
Pouvez-vous utiliser ce mot dans une phrase ?
Poo-vey voo u-tee-lee-zey suh moh dãn_zun frahz ?

How do you spell that word?
Comment on écrit ce mot ?
Koh-mãn õn_ney-kree suh moh ?

Go play with your brother.
Va jouer avec ton frère.
Vah zhoo-ey aa-vehk tõn frehr.

Come inside! It is dinnertime.
Rentrez ! C'est l'heure du dîner.
Rãn-trey ! Sey luhr du dee-ney.

Tell me about your day.
Parle-moi de ta journée.
Paarl mwah duh taa zhoor-ney.

Is there anywhere you want to go?
Tu veux aller quelque part ?
Tu vuh aa-ley kehl-kuh pahr ?

How are you feeling?
Comment tu te sens ?
Koh-mãn tu tuh sãn ?

What do you want me to make for dinner tonight?
Qu'est-ce que tu veux que je cuisine pour dîner ce soir ?
Kehs-kuh tu vuh kuh zhuh kwee-zeen poor dee-ney suh swahr ?

It's time for you to take a bath.
C'est l'heure de ton bain.
Sey luhr duh tõn bĩn.

Brush your teeth and wash behind your ears.
Brosse tes dents et lave derrière tes oreilles.
Brohs tey dãn ey laav deh-ree-ehr tey_zoh-reh-y.

You're not wearing that to bed.
Tu ne vas pas porter ça au lit.
Tu nuh vah pah pohr-tey sah oh lee.

I don't like the way you're dressed. Put something else on.
Je n'aime pas comment tu es habillé. Met quelque chose d'autre.
Zhuh nehm pah koh-mãn tu eh aa-bee-yey. Meh kehl-kuh shohz dohtr.

Did you make any friends today?
Tu as fait des nouveaux amis aujourd'hui ?
Tu ah feh dey noo-voh_zaa-mee oh-zhoor-dwee ?

Let me see your homework.
Fais-moi voir tes devoirs.
Feh mwah vwahr tey duh-vwahr.

Do I need to call your school?
Est-ce que je dois appeler ton école ?
Ehs-kuh zhuh dwah aa-puh-ley tõn_ney-kohl ?

The dog can't go outside right now.
Le chien ne peut pas sortir pour l'instant.
Luh shyĩn nuh puh pah sohr-teer poor lĩn-stãn.

Is the new quiz going to be available next week?
Est-ce que le nouveau quiz sera disponible la semaine prochaine ?
Ehs-kuh luh noo-voh kweez suh-rah dees-poh-neebl laa smehn proh-shehn ?

Are we allowed to use calculators with the test?
Est-ce qu'on a le droit d'utiliser des calculatrices pour le test ?
Ehs-kõn_nah luh drwah du-tee-lee-zey dey kaal-ku-laa-trees poor luh tehst ?

I would like to lead today's lesson.
J'aimerais animer la leçon d'aujourd'hui.
Zheh-muh-reh aa-nee-mey laa luh-sõn doh-zhoor-dwee.

I have a dorm curfew so I need to go back.
J'ai un couvre-feu dans le dortoir donc je dois retourner.
Zhey ũn koovr fuh dãn luh dohr-twahr dõnk zhuh dwah ruh-toor-ney.

Do I have to use pencil or ink?
Est-ce que je dois utiliser un crayon ou de l'encre ?
Ehs-kuh zhuh dwah u-tee-lee-zey ũn krey-õn oo duh lãnkr ?

Are cell phones allowed in class?
Les téléphones portables sont permis dans la classe ?
Ley tey-ley-fon pohr-taabl sõn pehr-mee dãn laa klaas ?

Where can I find the nearest dog park?
Où se trouve le parc pour chiens le plus proche ?
Oo suh troov luh paark poor shyĩn luh plu prohsh ?

Are dogs allowed to be off their leash here?
Est-ce qu'on a le droit d'enlever les laisses des chiens ici ?
Ehs-kõn_nah luh drwah dãn-luh-vey ley lehs dey shyĩn ee-see ?

Are children allowed here?
Est-ce que les enfants sont permis ici ?
Ehs-kuh ley_zãn-fãn sõn pehr-mee ee-see ?

I would like to set up a play date with our children.
J'aimerais arranger une journée pour nos enfants pour jouer ensemble.
Zheh-muh-reh aa-rãn-zhey un zhoor-ney poor noh_zãn-fãn poor zhoo-ey ãn-sãmbl.

I would like to invite you to my child's birthday party.
J'aimerais vous inviter à la fête d'anniversaire de mon enfant.
Zheh-muh-reh voo_zĩn-vee-tey aa laa feht daa-nee-vehr-sehr duh mõn_nãn-fãn.

Did you miss your dorm curfew last night?
Tu as raté le couvre-feu de ton dortoir hier soir ?
Tu ah raa-tey luh koovr fuh duh tõn dohr-twahr ee-yehr swahr ?

TRAVELER'S GUIDE

Over there is the library.
La bibliothèque est là-bas.
Laa bee-blee-oh-tehk eh laa-bah.

Just over there.
Juste là-bas.
Zhust laa-bah.

Yes, this way.
Oui, par ici.
Wee, paar ee-see.

I haven't done anything wrong.
Je n'ai rien fait de mal.
Zhuh ney ryĩn feh duh maal.

It was a misunderstanding.
C'était un mal-entendu.
Sey-teh_tũn maal-ãn-tãn-du.

I am an American citizen.
Je suis un citoyen américain.
Zhuh swee_zũn see-twah-yĩn aa-mey-ree-kĩn.

We are tourists on vacation.
Nous sommes des touristes en vacances.
Noo sohm dey too-reest ãn vaa-kãns.

I am looking for an apartment.
Je suis à la recherche d'un appartement.
Zhuh swee_zaa laa ruh-shehr-sh dũn_naa-paar-tuh-mãn.

This is a short-term stay.
C'est pour un séjour de courte durée.
Sey poor ũn sey-zhoor duh koort du-rey.

I am looking for a place to rent.
Je suis à la recherche d'un lieu à louer.
Zhuh swee_zaa laa ruh-shehr-sh dũn lyuh aa loo-ey.

Where can we grab a quick bite to eat?
Où est-ce qu'on peut s'acheter une bouchée rapide ?
Oo ehs-kõn puh saa-shuh-tey un boo-shey raa-peed ?

We need the cheapest place you can find.
On a besoin du lieu le moins cher que vous pouvez trouver.
Õn ah buh-zwĩn du lyuh luh mwĩn shehr kuh voo poo-vey troo-vey.

Do you have a map of the city?
Avez-vous une carte de la ville ?
Aa-vey voo un kaart duh laa veel ?

What places do tourists usually visit when they come here?
Où est-ce que les touristes restent d'habitude quand ils viennent ici ?
Oo ehs-kuh ley too-reest rehst daa-bee-tud kãn_teel vyehn ee-see ?

Can you take our picture, please?
Pouvez-vous nous prendre notre photo, s'il vous plaît ?
Poo-vey voo noo prãndr nohtre foh-toh, seel voo pleh ?

Do you take foreign credit cards?
Est-ce que vous acceptez les cartes de crédit étrangères ?
Ehs-kuh voo_zaak-sehp-tey ley kaart duh krey-dee ey-trãn-zhehr ?

I would like to hire a bicycle to take us around the city.
J'aimerais louer un vélo pour qu'on fasse le tour de la ville.
Zheh-muh-reh loo-ey ũn vey-loh poor kõn fahs luh toor duh laa veel.

Do you mind if I take pictures here?
Ça vous dérange si je prends des photos ici ?
Saa voo dey-rãnzh see zhuh prãn dey foh-toh ee-see ?

ANSWERS

Yes, to some extent.
Oui, à un certain point.
Wee, aa ũn sehr-tĩn pwĩn.

I'm not sure.
Je ne suis pas sûr.
Zhuh nuh swee pah sur.

Yes, go ahead.
Oui, vas-y.
Wee, vah_zee.

Yes, just like you.
Oui, comme vous.
Wee, kom voo.

No, no problem at all.
Non, aucun problème du tout.
Nõn, oh-kũn proh-blehm du too.

This is a little more expensive than the other item.
Celui-ci est un peu plus cher que l'autre article.
Suh-lwee see eh_tũn puh plu shehr kuh lohtr aar-teekl.

My city is small but nice.
Ma ville est petite mais agréable.
Maa veel eh puh-teet meh aa-grey-aabl.

This city is quite big.
Cette ville est assez grande.
Seht veel eh_taa-sey grãnd.

I'm from America.
Je viens de l'Amérique.
Zhuh vyĩn duh laa-mey-reek.

We'll wait for you.
On va vous attendre.
Õn vah voo_zaa-tãndr.

I love going for walks.
J'aime me promener.
Zhehm muh proh-muh-ney.

I'm a woman.
Je suis une femme.
Zhuh swee_zun faam.

Good, I'm going to see it.
Super, je vais le voir.
Su-pehr, zhuh veh luh vwahr.

So do I.
Moi aussi.
Mwah oh-see.

I'll think about it and call you tomorrow with an answer.
Je vais y réfléchir, et je vous appellerais demain pour vous donner une réponse.
Zhuh veh_zee rey-fley-sheer, ey zhuh voo_zaa-pehl-reh duh-mĩn poor voo doh-ney un rey-põns.

I have two children.
J'ai deux enfants.
Zhey duh_zãn-fãn.

Does this place have a patio?
Est-ce qu'il y a une terrasse ici ?
Ehs-keel ee yah un tey-raas ee-see ?

No, the bathroom is vacant.
Non, il n'y a personne dans la salle de bain.
Nõn, eel nee-yah pehr-sohn dãn laa saal duh bĩn.

I'm not old enough.
Je n'ai pas l'âge qu'il faut.
Zhuh ney pah lahzh keel foh.

No, it is very easy.
Non, c'est très facile.
Nõn, sey treh faa-seel.

Understood.
C'est compris.
Sey kõm-pree.

Only if you go first.
Seulement si tu y vas en premier.
Suhl-mãn see tu ee vah ãn pruh-myey.

Yes, that is correct.
Oui, c'est ça.
Wee, sey sah.

That was the wrong answer.
Ce n'était pas la bonne réponse.
Suh ney-teh pah laa bon rey-põns.

We haven't decided yet.
On n'a pas encore décidé.
Õn_nah pah_zãn-kahr dey-see-dey.

We can try.
On peut essayer.
Õn puh eh-sey-ey.

I like to read books.
J'aime lire les livres.
Zhehm leer ley leevr.

We can go there together.
On peut y aller ensemble.
Õn puh ee aa-ley ãn-sãmbl.

Yes, I see.
Oui, je vois.
Wee, zhuh vwah.

That looks interesting.
Ça a l'air intéressant.
Saa ah lehr ĩn-tey-reh-sãn.

Me neither.
Moi non plus.
Mwah nõn plu.

It was fun.
C'était amusant.
Sey-teh aa-mu-zãn.

Me too.
Moi aussi.
Mwah oh-see.

Stay there.
Restez-là.
Rehs-tey lah.

We were worried about you.
On s'inquiétait pour vous.
Õn sĩn-kee-ey-teh poor voo.

No, not really.
Non, pas vraiment.
Nõn, pah vreh-mãn.

Unbelievable.
Incroyable.
Ĩn-krwah-yaabl.

No, I didn't make it in time.
Non, je suis pas arrivé à temps.
Nõn, zhuh swee pah aa-ree-vey aa tãn.

No, you cannot.
Non, vous ne pouvez pas.
Nõn, voo nuh poo-vey pah.

Here you go.
Tenez.
Tuh-ney.

It was good.
C'était bon.
Sey-teh bõn.

Ask my wife.
Demandez à ma femme.
Duh-mãn-dey aa maa faam.

That's up to him.
C'est à lui de voir.
Sey_taa lwee duh vwahr.

That is not allowed.
C'est interdit.
Sey_tĩn-tehr-dee.

You can stay at my place.
Vous pouvez rester chez moi.
Voo poo-vey rehs-tey shey mwah.

Only if you want to.
Seulement si vous voulez.
Suhl-mãn see voo voo-ley.

It depends on my schedule.
Ça dépend de mon horaire.
Saa dey-pãn duh mõn_noh-rehr.

I don't think that's possible.
Je crois pas que ça sera possible.
Zhuh krwah pah kuh saa suh-rah poh-seebl.

You're not bothering me.
Vous me dérangez pas.
Voo muh dey-rãn-zhey pah.

139

The salesman will know.

Le vendeur va le savoir.

Luh vãn-duhr vah luh saa-vwahr.

I have to work.

Je dois travailler.

Zhuh dwah traa-vah-yey.

I'm late.

Je suis en retard.

Zhuh swee_zãn ruh-tahr.

To pray.

Pour prier.

Poor pree-ey.

I'll do my best.

Je ferais de mon mieux.

Zhuh fuh-reh duh mõn myuh.

DIRECTIONS

Over here.
Par ici.
Paar ee-see.

Go straight ahead.
Allez tout droit.
Aa-ley too drwah.

Follow the straight line.
Suivez la ligne droite.
Swee-vey laa leen drwaht.

Go halfway around the circle.
Faites le demi-tour du cercle.
Feht luh duh-mee toor du sehrkl.

It is to the left.
C'est à gauche.
Sey_taa gohsh.

Where is the party going to be?
Où est-ce que la fête aura lieu ?
Oo ehs-kuh laa feht oh-rah lyuh ?

Where is the library situated?
Où se trouve la bibliothèque ?
Oo suh troov laa bee-blee-oh-tehk ?

It is to the north.
C'est au nord.
Sey_toh nohr.

You can find it down the street.
Vous le trouverez au bout de la rue.
Voo luh troo-vuh-rey oh boo duh laa ru.

Go into the city to get there.
Rentrez dans la ville pour y accèder.
Rãn-trey dãn laa veel poor ee aak-seh-dey.

Where are you now?
Où êtes-vous maintenant ?
Oo eht voo mĩn-tuh-nãn ?

There is a fire hydrant right in front of me.
Il y a une borne d'incendie directement devant moi.
Eel ee yah un bohrn dĩn-sãn-dee dee-rehk-tuh-mãn duh-vãn mwah.

Do you know a shortcut?
Connaissez-vous un raccourci ?
Koh-neh-sey voo ũn raa-koor-see ?

Where is the freeway?
Où se trouve l'autoroute ?
Oo suh troov loh-toh-root ?

Do I need exact change for the toll?
Est-ce que j'ai besoin de la monnaie exacte pour le péage ?
Ehs-kuh zheh buh-zwĩn duh laa moh-neh ehg-zaakt poor luh pey-aazh ?

At the traffic light, turn right.
Tournez à droite au feu de circulation.
Toor-ney aa drwaht oh fuh duh seer-ku-laa-syõn.

When you get to the intersection, turn left.
Tournez à gauche lorsque vous arrivez à l'intersection.
Toor-ney aa gohsh lohr-skuh voo_zaa-ree-vey aa lĩn-tehr-sehk-syõn.

Stay in your lane until it splits off to the right.
Restez dans votre voie jusqu'à ce qu'il vire à droite.
Reh-stey dãn vohtr vwah jus-kaa_skeel veer aa drwaht.

Don't go onto the ramp.
Ne prenez pas la bretelle.
Nuh pruh-ney pah laa bruh-tehl.

You are going in the wrong direction.
Vous allez dans le mauvais sens.
Voo_zaa-ley dãn luh moh-vey sãns.

Can you guide me to this location?
Pouvez-vous me guider à cet endroit ?
Poo-vey voo muh gee-dey aa seh_tãn-drwah ?

Stop at the crossroads.
Arrêtez à la croisée des chemins.
Aa-reh-tey aa laa krwah-zey dey shuh-mĩn.

You missed our turn. Please turn around.
Vous avez raté notre virage. S'il vous plaît faites demi-tour.
Voo_zaa-vey raa-tey nohtr vee-razh. Seel voo pleh feht duh-mee toor.

It is illegal to turn here.
C'est interdit de tourner ici.
Sey_tĩn-tehr-dee duh toor-ney ee-see.

We're lost, could you help us?
Nous sommes perdus, pouvez-vous nous aider ?
Noo som pehr-du, poo-vey voo noo_zey-dey ?

APOLOGIES

Dad, I'm sorry.
Je suis désolé, Papa.
Zhuh swee dey-zoh-ley, pah-pah.

I apologize for being late.
Je m'excuse pour le retard.
Zhuh mehk-skuz poor luh ruh-tahr.

Excuse me for not bringing money.
Je m'excuse de ne pas avoir emmené de l'argent.
Zhuh mehk-skuz duh nuh pah_zaa-vwahr ah-muh-ney duh laar-zhãn.

That was my fault.
C'était de ma faute.
Sey-tey duh maa foht.

It won't happen again, I'm sorry.
Ça n'arrivera pas une deuxième fois, je suis navré.
Saa naa-ree-vrah pah un duh-zyehm fwah, zhuh swee nah-vrey.

I won't break another promise.
Je ne briserais pas une autre promesse.
Zhuh nuh bree-zuh-reh pah_zun_nohtr proh-mehs.

You have my word that I'll be careful.
Vous avez ma parole que je ferais attention.
Voo_zaa-vey maa paa-rohl kuh zhuh fuh-reh aa-tãn-syõn.

I'm sorry, I wasn't paying attention.
Je suis désolé, je ne faisais pas attention.
Zhuh swee dey-zoh-ley, zhuh nuh fuh-zeh pah aa-tãn-syõn.

I regret that. I'm so sorry.
Je le regrette. Je suis tellement désolé.
Zhuh luh ruh-greht. Zhuh swee tehl-mãn dey-zoh-ley.

I'm sorry, but today I can't.
Je suis désolé, mais je ne peux pas aujourd'hui.
Zhuh swee dey-zoh-ley, meh zhuh nuh puh pah oh-zhoor-dwee.

It's not your fault, I'm sorry.
Ce n'est pas votre faute, je suis désolé.
Suh ney pah vohtr foht, zhuh swee dey-zoh-ley.

Please, give me another chance.
S'il vous plaît, donnez-moi une autre chance.
Seel voo pleh, doh-ney mwah un_nohtr shãns.

Will you ever forgive me?
Pourriez-vous me pardonner un jour ?
Poo-ree-ey voo muh paar-doh-ney ũn zhoor ?

I hope in time we can still be friends.
J'espère qu'un jour on pourra être amis de nouveau.
Zheh-spehr kũn zhoor õn poo-rah ehtr aa-mee duh noo-voh.

I screwed up, and I'm sorry.
J'ai mal fait, et je m'excuse.
Zhey maal feh, ey zhuh mehk-skuz.

SMALL TALK

No.
Non.
Nõn.

Yes.
Oui.
Wee.

Okay.
D'accord.
Daa-kohr.

Please.
S'il vous plaît.
Seel voo pleh.

Do you fly out of the country often?
Vous prenez souvent des vols à l'étranger ?
Voo pruh-ney soo-vãn dey vohl aa ley-trãn-zhey ?

Thank you.
Merci.
Mehr-see.

That's okay.
Pas de problème.
Pah duh proh-blehm.

I went shopping.
Je suis parti faire du shopping.
Zhuh swee paar-tee fehr du shoh-peeng.

There.
Voilà.
Vwah-lah.

Very well.
D'accord.
Daa-kohr.

What?
Pardon ?
Paar-dõn ?

I think you'll like it.
Je crois que ça va vous plaire.
Zhuh krwah kuh saa vah voo plehr.

When?
Quand ?
Kãn ?

I didn't sleep well.
Je n'ai pas bien dormi.
Zhuh ney pah byĩn dohr-mee.

Until what time?
Jusqu'à quelle heure ?
Zhu-skaa kehl uhr ?

We are waiting in line.
On fait la queue.
Õn feh laa kuh.

We're only waiting for a little bit longer.
On ne va pas attendre beaucoup plus longtemps.
Õn nuh vah pah aa-tãndr boh-koo plu lõn-tãn.

How?
Comment ?
Koh-mãn ?

Where?
Où ?
Oo ?

I'm glad.
Je suis content.
Zhuh swee kõn-tãn.

You are very tall.
Vous êtes très grand.
Voo_zeht treh grãn.

I like to speak your language.
J'aime bien parler votre langue.
Zhehm byĩn paar-ley vohtr lãng.

You are very kind.
Vous êtes très gentil.
Voo_zeht treh zhãn-tee.

Happy birthday!
Joyeux anniversaire !
Zhwah-yuh_zaa-nee-vehr-sehr !

I would like to thank you very much.
J'aimerais vous remercier à fond.
Zheh-muh-reh voo ruh-mehr-see-ey aa fõn.

Here is a gift that I bought for you.
Voici un cadeau que je vous ai acheté.
Vwah-see ũn kaa-doh kuh zhuh voo_zey aash-tey.

Yes. Thank you for all of your help.
Oui. Merci pour tout votre aide.
Wee. Mehr-see poor too voht_rehd.

What did you get?
Qu'est-ce que vous avez pris ?
Keh-skuh voo_zaa-vey pree ?

Have a good trip!
Bon voyage !
Bõn vwah-yaazh !

148

This place is very special to me.
Cet endroit m'est très précieux.
Seh_tãn-drwah meh treh prey-syuh.

My foot is asleep.
J'ai les fourmis dans le pied.
Zhey ley foor-mee dãn luh pyey.

May I open this now or later?
Je peux l'ouvrir maintenant ou je le fais plus tard ?
Zhuh puh loo-vreer mĩn-tuh-nãn oo zhuh luh feh plu tahr ?

Why do you think that is?
Pourquoi pensez-vous que c'est le cas ?
Poor-kwah pãn-sey voo kuh sey luh kah ?

Which do you like better, chocolate or caramel?
Lequel préférez-vous, le chocolat ou le caramel ?
Luh-kehl prey-fey-rey voo, luh shoh-koh-lah oo luh kaa-raa-mehl ?

Be safe on your journey.
Faites attention en voyageant.
Feht_zaa-tãn-syõn ãn vwah-ya-zhãn.

I want to do this for a little longer.
Je veux faire ça un peu plus longtemps.
Zhuh vuh fehr sah ũn puh plu lõn-tãn.

This is a picture that I took at the hotel.
Voici une photo que j'ai pris à l'hôtel.
Vwah-see un foh-toh kuh zhey pree aa loh-tehl.

Allow me.
Permettez-moi.
Pehr-meh-tey mwah.

I was surprised.
J'étais surpris.
Zhey-teh sur-pree.

I like that.
J'aime ça.
Zhehm sah.

Are you in high spirits today?
Vous êtes de bonne humeur aujourd'hui ?
Voo_zeht duh bon u-muhr oh-zhoor-dwee ?

Oh, here comes my wife.
Ah, voilà ma femme qui arrive.
Ah, vwah-lah maa faam kee aa-reev.

Can I see the photograph?
Je peux voir la photo ?
Zhuh puh vwahr laa foh-toh ?

Feel free to ask me anything.
N'hésitez pas à me demander quoi que ce soit.
Ney-zee-tey pah aa muh duh-mãn-dey kwah kuh suh swah.

That was magnificent!
C'était magnifique !
Sey-tey maa-nyee-feek !

See you some other time.
À la prochaine.
Aa laa proh-shehn.

No more, please.
Ça suffit, merci.
Saa su-fee, mehr-see.

Please don't use that.
S'il vous plaît n'utilisez pas cela.
Seel voo pleh nu-tee-lee-zey pah suh-lah.

That is very pretty.
C'est très joli ça.
Sey treh zhoh-lee sah.

Would you say that again?
Pouvez-vous répéter cela ?
Poo-vey voo rey-pey-tey suh-lah ?

Speak slowly.
Parlez lentement.
Paar-ley lãn-tuh-mãn.

I'm home.
Je suis de retour à la maison.
Zhuh swee duh ruh-toor aa laa meh-zõn.

Is this your home?
C'est votre maison ?
Sey vohtr meh-zõn ?

I know a lot about the area.
Je connais beaucoup sur la région.
Zhuh koh-neh boh-koo sur laa rey-zhyõn.

Welcome back. How was your day?
Bienvenue. Comment s'est passé ta journée ?
Byĩn-vuh-nu. Koh-mãn sey pah-sey taa zhoor-ney ?

I read every day.
Je lis tous les jours.
Zhuh lee too ley zhoor.

My favorite type of book is novels by Stephen King.
Mon genre de livre préféré c'est les romans par Stephen King.
Mõn zhãnr duh leevr prey-fey-rey sey ley roh-mãn paar stee-faan keeng.

You surprised me!
Vous m'avez surpris !
Voo maa-vey sur-pree !

I am short on time so I have to go.
Je n'ai pas beaucoup de temps donc je dois partir.
Zhuh ney pah boh-koo duh tãn dõnk zhuh dwah paar-teer.

Thank you for having this conversation.
Merci d'avoir participé à cette discussion.
Mehr-see daa-vwahr paar-tee-see-pey aa seht dees-ku-syõn.

Oh, when is it?
Ah, c'est quand ?
Ah, sey kãn ?

This is my brother, Jeremy.
Ça c'est mon frère, Jérémie.
Sah sey mõn frehr, zhey-rey-mee.

That is my favorite bookstore.
Ça c'est ma librairie préférée.
Sah sey maa lee-breh-ree prey-fey-rey.

That statue is bigger than it looks.
Cette statue est plus grande qu'on dirait.
Seht staa-tu eh plu grãnd kõn dee-reh.

Look at the shape of that cloud!
Regardez la forme de ce nuage !
Ruh-gaar-dey laa fohr-m duh suh nu-aazh !

BUSINESS

I am president of the credit union.
Je suis le président de la coopérative de crédit.
Zhuh swee luh prey-zee-dãn duh laa coh-oh-pey-raa-teev duh krey-dee.

We are expanding in your area.
Nous élargissons dans votre région.
Noo_zey-laar-zhee-sõn dãn vohtr rey-zhyõn.

I am looking for work in the agriculture field.
Je cherche du travail dans le domaine agriculturel.
Zhuh shehr-sh du traa-vah-y dãn luh doh-mehn aa-gree-kul-tu-rehl.

Sign here, please.
Signez ici, s'il vous plaît.
See-nyey ee-see, seel voo pleh.

I am looking for temporary work.
Je cherche du travail temporaire.
Zhuh shehr-sh du traa-vah-y tãm-poh-rehr.

I need to call and set up that meeting.
Je dois appeler pour organiser cette réunion.
Zhuh dwah aa-puh-ley poor ohr-gaa-nee-zey seht rey-u-nyõn.

Is the line open?
Est-ce que la ligne est ouverte ?
Ehs-kuh laa lee-ny eh_too-vehrt ?

I need you to hang up the phone.
J'ai besoin que vous raccrochiez le téléphone.
Zhey buh-zwĩn kuh voo raa-kroh-shyey luh tey-ley-fohn.

Who should I ask for more information about your business?
Avec qui je peux me renseigner sur votre entreprise ?
Aa-vehk kee zhuh puh muh rãn-seh-nyey sur vohtr ãn-truh-preez ?

There was no answer when you handed me the phone.
Il n'y avait personne lorsque vous m'avez passé le téléphone.
Eel nee_yaa-veh pehr-sohn lohr-skuh voo maa-vey pah-sey luh tey-ley-fohn.

Robert is not here at the moment.
Robert n'est pas là à l'instant.
Roh-behr neh pah lah aa lĩn-stãn.

Call me after work, thanks.
Appelez-moi après le travail, merci.
Aa-puh-ley mwah aa-preh luh traa-vah-y, mehr-see.

We're strongly considering your contract offer.
Nous considérons sérieusement votre offre de contrat.
Noo kõn-see-dey-rõn sey-ryuhz-mãn vohtr ohfr duh kõn-trah.

Have the necessary forms been signed yet?
Est-ce que les formulaires nécessaires ont été signés ou pas encore ?
Ehs-kuh ley fohr-mu-lehr ney-sey-sehr õn ey-tey see-nyey oo pah_zãn-kahr ?

I have a few hours available after work.
J'ai quelques heures de disponibles après le travail.
Zhey kehl-kuh_zuhr duh dee-spoh-neebl aa-preh luh traa-vah-y.

What do they make there?
Qu'est-ce qu'ils fabriquent là ?
Kehs-keel faa-breek lah ?

I have no tasks assigned to me.
On ne m'a attribué aucune tâche.
Õn nuh mah aa-tree-bu-ey oh-kun tahsh.

How many workers are they hiring?
Combien ils embauchent d'ouvriers ?
Kõm-byĩn eel_zãm-bohsh doo-vree-ey ?

It should take me three hours to complete this task.
Ça devrait me prendre trois heures pour terminer cette tâche.
Saa duh-vreh muh prândr trwah_zuhr poor tehr-mee-ney seht tahsh.

Don't use that computer, it is only for financial work.
N'utilisez pas cet ordinateur, c'est seulement pour les travaux financiers.
Nu-tee-lee-zey pah seht ohr-dee-naa-tuhr, sey suhl-mãn poor ley traa-voh fee-nãn-see-ey.

I only employ people that I can rely on.
Je n'embauche que les gens sur qui je peux compter.
Zhuh nãm-bohsh kuh ley zhãn sur kee zhuh puh kõn-tey.

After I talk to my lawyers, we can discuss this further.
On peut en discuter davantage lorsque j'aurais parlé avec mes avocats.
Õn puh ãn dees-ku-tey daa-vãn-taazh lohr-skuh zhoh-reh paar-ley aa-vehk mey_zaa-voh-kah.

Are there any open positions in my field?
Y-a-t-il des postes libres dans mon domaine ?
Ee-yah teel dey pohst leebr dãn mõn doh-mehn ?

I'll meet you in the conference room.
Je vous retrouve dans la salle de conférence.
Zhuh voo ruh-troov dãn laa saal duh kõn-fey-rãns.

Call and leave a message on my office phone.
Appelez et laissez un message sur mon téléphone de bureau.
Aa-puh-ley ey leh-sey ũn meh-saazh sur mõn tey-ley-fon duh bu-roh.

Send me a fax with that information.
Envoyez-moi une télécopie avec cette information.
Ãn-vwah-yey mwah un tey-ley-koh-pee aa-vehk seht ĩn-fohr-maa-syõn.

Hi, I would like to leave a message for Sheila.
Bonjour, j'aimerais laisser un message pour Sheila.
Bõn-zhoor, zheh-muh-reh leh-sey ũn meh-saazh poor shee-lah.

Please repeat your last name.
S'il vous plaît répètez votre nom de famille.
Seel voo pleh rey-peh-tey vohtr nõn duh faa-mee-y.

I would like to buy wholesale.
J'aimerais acheter en gros.
Zheh-muh-reh aa-shuh-tey ãn groh.

How do you spell your last name?
Comment écrivez-vous votre nom de famille ?
Koh-mãn ey-kree-vey voo vohtr nõn duh faa-mee-y ?

I called your boss yesterday and left a message.
J'ai appelé votre chef hier, et j'ai laissé un message.
Zhey aa-puh-ley vohtr shehf ee-ehr, ey zhey leh-sey ũn meh-saazh.

That customer hung up on me.
Ce client m'a raccroché au nez.
Suh klee-ãn mah raa-kroh-shey oh ney.

She called but didn't leave a callback number.
Elle a appelé, mais elle n'a pas laissé un numéro de rappel.
Ehl ah aa-puh-ley meh ehl nah pah leh-sey ũn nu-mey-roh duh raa-pehl.

Hello! Am I speaking to Bob?
Bonjour ! Je parle avec Bob ?
Bõn-zhoor ! Zhuh paarl aa-vehk bohb ?

Excuse me, but could you speak up? I can't hear you.
Pardon, mais vous pouvez parler plus fort ? Je ne vous entends pas.
Paar-dõn, meh voo poo-vey paar-ley plu fohr ? Zhuh nuh voo_zãn-tãn pah.

The line is very bad, could you move to a different area so I can hear you better?
Le réseau est très mauvais, vous pouvez vous deplacer un peu pour que je puisse vous entendre mieux ?
Luh rey-zoh eh treh moh-veh, voo poo-vey voo dey-plaa-sey ũn puh poor kuh zhuh pwees voo_zãn-tãndr myuh ?

I would like to apply for a work visa.
J'aimerais déposer une demande pour un visa de travail.
Zheh-muh-reh dey-poh-zey un duh-mãnd poor ũn vee-zah duh traa-vah-y.

It is my dream to work here teaching the language.
C'est mon rêve de travailler ici et enseigner la langue.
Sey mõn rehv duh traa-vah-yey ee-see ey ãn-seh-nyey laa lãn-g.

I have always wanted to work here.
J'ai toujours voulu travailler ici.
Zhey too-zhoor voo-lu traa-vah-yey ee-see.

Where do you work?
Où travaillez-vous ?
Oo traa-vah-yey voo ?

Are we in the same field of work?
Travaillons-nous dans le même domaine ?
Traa-vah-yõn noo dãn luh mehm doh-mehn ?

Do we share an office?
On partage un bureau ?
Õn paar-taazh ũn bu-roh ?

What do you do for a living?
C'est quoi votre métier ?
Sey kwah vohtr mey-tyey ?

I work in the city as an engineer for Cosco.
Je travaille dans la ville comme ingénieur pour Cosco.
Zhuh traa-vah-y dãn laa veel kohm ĩn-zhey-nyuhr poor kohs-koh.

I am an elementary teacher.
Je suis enseignant au primaire.
Zhuh swee_zãn-sey-nyãn oh pree-mehr.

What time should I be at the meeting?
À quelle heure je devrais être à la réunion ?
Aa kehl uhr zhuh duh-vreh ehtr aa laa rey-u-nyõn ?

Would you like me to catch you up on what the meeting was about?
Voulez-vous que je vous mette à jour sur le sujet de la réunion ?
Voo-ley voo kuh zhuh voo meht aa zhoor sur luh su-zheh duh laa rey-u-nyõn ?

I would like to set up a meeting with your company.
J'aimerais organiser une réunion avec votre société.
Zheh-muh-reh ohr-gaa-nee-zey un rey-u-nyõn aa-vehk vohtr soh-syey-tey.

Please, call my secretary for that information.
S'il vous plaît appelez mon secrétaire pour cette information.
Seel voo pleh aa-puh-ley mõn suh-krey-tehr poor seht ĩn-fohr-maa-syõn.

I will have to ask my lawyer.
Je vais devoir demander à mon avocat.
Zhuh veh duh-vwahr duh-mãn-dey aa mõn_naa-voh-kah.

Fax it over to my office number.
Envoyez-le par télécopieur au numéro de mon bureau.
Ãn-vwah-yey luh paar tey-ley-koh-pee-uhr oh nu-mey-roh duh mõn bu-roh.

Will I have any trouble calling into the office?
Est-ce que j'aurais des difficultés à appeler le bureau ?
Ehs-kuh zhoh-reh dey dee-fee-kul-tey aa aa-puh-ley luh bu-roh ?

Do you have a business card I can have?
Avez-vous une carte de visite que vous pourriez me donner ?
Aa-vey voo un kaart duh vee-zeet kuh voo poo-ryey muh doh-ney ?

Here is my business card. Please, take it.
Voici ma carte de visite. S'il vous plaît prenez-le.
Vwah-see maa kaart duh vee-zeet. Seel voo pleh pruh-ney luh.

My colleague and I are going to lunch.
Je vais déjeuner avec mon collègue.
Zhuh veh dey-zhuh-ney aa-vehk mõn koh-lehg.

I am the director of finance for my company.
Je suis le directeur financier de ma société.
Zhuh swee luh dee-rehk-tuhr fee-nãn-syey duh maa soh-syey-tey.

I manage the import goods of my company.
Je gère l'importation des biens pour ma société.
Zhuh zhehr lĩn-pohr-taa-syõn dey byĩn poor maa soh-syey-tey.

My colleagues' boss is Steven.
Le chef de mes collègues s'appelle Steven.
Luh shehf duh mey koh-lehg saa-pehl stee-vehn.

I work for the gas station company.
Je travaille pour la société gazière.
Zhuh traa-vah-y poor laa soh-syey-tey gah-zyehr.

What company do you work for?
Vous travaillez pour quelle société ?
Voo traa-vah-yey poor kehl soh-syey-tey ?

I'm an independent contractor.
Je suis un entrepreneur indépendant.
Zhuh swee_zŭn ãn-truh-pruh-nuhr ĩn-dey-pãn-dãn.

How many employees do you have at your company?
Combien y-a-t-il de salariés dans votre société ?
Kõm-byĩn ee-yah teel duh saa-laa-ryey dãn vohtr soh-syey-tey ?

I know a lot about engineering.
Je connais beaucoup sur l'ingénierie.
Zhuh koh-neh boh-koo sur lĩn-zhey-nee-yuh-ree.

I can definitely resolve that dispute for you.
Je peux certainement vous résoudre ce conflit.
Zhuh puh sehr-tehn-mãn voo rey-zoodr suh kõn-flee.

You should hire an interpreter.
Vous devriez embaucher un interprète.
Voo duh-vree-ey ãm-boh-shey ŭn ĩn-tehr-preht.

Are you hiring any additional workers?
Embauchez-vous d'autres ouvriers ?
Ãm-boh-shey voo dohtr oo-vree-ey ?

How much experience do I need to work here?
Combien il me faut d'expérience pour travailler ici ?
Kõm-byĩn eel muh foh dehks-pey-ryãns poor traa-vah-yey ee-see ?

Our marketing manager handles that.
Notre responsable de marketing gère cela.
Nohtr rehs-põn-saabl duh mahr-kuh-teeng zhehr suh-lah.

I would like to poach one of your workers.
J'aimerais débaucher un de vos ouvriers.
Zheh-muh-reh dey-boh-shey ũn duh voh_zoo-vree-ey.

Can we work out a deal that is beneficial for the both of us?
Pouvons-nous négocier un accord qui nous bénéficie tout les deux ?
Poo-võn noo ney-goh-syey ũn_naa-kohr kee noo bey-ney-fee-see too ley duh ?

My resources are at your disposal.
Mes ressources sont à votre disposition.
Mey ruh-soors sõn_taa vohtr dees-poh-zee-syõn.

I am afraid that we have to let you go.
Je crains que, malheureusement, on doit vous lâcher.
Zhuh krĩn kuh, maal-uh-ruhz-mãn, õn dwah voo lah-shey.

This is your first warning. Please don't do that again.
C'est votre premier avertissement. S'il vous plaît ne le refaites pas.
Sey vohtr pruh-myeh_raa-vehr-tees-mãn. Seel voo pleh nuh luh ruh-feht pah.

File a complaint with HR about the incident.
Déposez une plainte avec le responsable RH à propos de l'incident.
Dey-poh-zey un plĩnt aa-vehk luh rehs-põn-saabl ehr-aash aa proh-poh duh lĩn-see-dãn.

Who is showing up for our lunch meeting?
Qui va assister à la réunion de déjeuner ?
Kee vah aa-see-stey aa laa rey-u-nyõn duh dey-zhuh-ney ?

Clear out the rest of my day.
Dégagez le reste de mon calendrier pour la journée.
Dey-gaa-zhey luh rehst duh mõn kaa-lãn-dree-ey poor laa zhour-ney.

We need to deposit this into the bank.
On doit déposer ça dans la banque.
Õn dwah dey-poh-zey sah dãn laa bãnk.

Can you cover the next hour for me?
Pouvez-vous prendre ma place pendant l'heure suivante ?
Poo-vey voo prãndr maa plaas pãn-dãn luhr swee-vãnt ?

If Shania calls, please push her directly through.
Si Shania appelle, s'il vous plaît passez-la-moi directement.
See shah-nyah aa-pehl, seel voo pleh pah-sey laa mwah dee-rehk-tuh-mãn.

I'm leaving early today.
Je pars tôt aujourd'hui.
Zhuh pahr toh oh-zhoor-dwee.

I'll be working late tonight.
Je vais rester tard au travail ce soir.
Zhuh veh rehs-tey tahr oh traa-vah-y suh swahr.

You can use the bathroom in my office.
Vous pouvez utiliser la salle de bain dans mon bureau.
Voo poo-vey u-tee-lee-zey laa saal duh bĩn dãn mõn bu-roh.

You can use my office phone to call out.
Vous pouvez utiliser mon téléphone de bureau pour passer un appel.
Voo poo-vey u-tee-lee-zey mõn tey-ley-fon duh bu-roh poor pah-sey ũn_naa-pehl.

Please, close the door behind you.
S'il vous plaît fermez la porte derrière vous.
Seel voo pleh fehr-mey laa pohrt deh-ree-ehr voo.

I need to talk to you privately.
J'ai besoin de vous parler en privé.
Zhey buh-zwĩn duh voo pahr-ley ãn pree-vey.

Your team is doing good work on this project.
Votre équipe fait du bon travail sur ce projet.
Vohtr ey-keep feh du bõn traa-vah-y sur suh proh-zheh.

Our numbers are down this quarter.
Nos chiffres ont baissé ce trimestre.
Noh sheefr õn bey-sey suh tree-mehstr.

I need you to work harder than usual.

J'ai besoin que vous mettiez plus d'effort que d'habitude.

Zhey buh-zwĩn kuh voo meh-tee-ey plus deh-fohr kuh daa-bee-tud.

I'm calling in sick today. Can anyone cover my shift?

Je prends un congé de maladie aujourd'hui. Y-a-t-il quelqu'un qui peut me remplacer ?

Zhuh prãn ũn kõn-zhey duh maa-laa-dee oh-zhoor-dwee. Ee-yah-teel kehl-kũn kee puh muh rãm-plaa-sey ?

Tom, we are thinking of promoting you.

Tom, on pense à vous faire une promotion.

Tom, õn pãns aa voo fehr un proh-moh-syõn.

I would like a raise.

J'aimerais avoir une augmentation de salaire.

Zheh-muh-reh aa-vwahr un ohg-mãn-taa-syõn duh saa-lehr.

THE WEATHER

I think the weather is changing.
Je crois que le temps va changer.
Zhuh krwah kuh luh tãn vah shãn-zhey.

Be careful, it is raining outside.
Faites attention, il pleut dehors.
Feht aa-tãn-syõn, eel pluh duh-ohr.

Make sure to bring your umbrella
N'oubliez pas de prendre votre parapluie.
Noo-blee-ey pah duh prãndr vohtr paa-raa-plwee.

Get out of the rain or you will catch a cold.
Sortez de la pluie, si non vous allez attraper la grippe.
Sohr-tey duh laa plwee, see nõn voo_zaa-ley aa-traa-pey laa greep.

Is it snowing?
Il neige ?
Eel nehzh ?

The snow is very thick right now.
La neige est très épaisse à l'instant.
Laa nehzh eh treh_zey-pehs aa lĩn-stãn.

Be careful, the road is full of ice.
Attention, la rue est très glacée.
Aa-tãn-syõn, laa ru eh treh glaa-sey.

What is the climate like here? Is it warm or cold?
C'est quoi le climat ici ? Il fait chaud ou froid ?
Sey kwah luh klee-mah ee-see ? Eel feh shoh oo frwah ?

It has been a very nice temperature here.
La température a été très agreable ici.
Laa tãm-pey-raa-tur ah ey-tey treh_zaa-grey-aabl ee-see.

Does it rain a lot here?
Est-ce qu'il pleut beaucoup ici ?
Ehs-keel pluh boh-koo ee-see ?

The temperature is going to break records this week.
La température va battre des records cette semaine.
Laa tãm-pey-raa-tur vah baatr dey ruh-kohr seht suh-mehn.

Does it ever snow here?
Est-ce qu'il neige parfois ici ?
Ehs-keel nehzh paar-fwah ee-see.

When does it get sunny?
Quand est-ce qu'il fait soleil ?
Kãn_tehs-keel feh soh-leh-y ?

What's the forecast look like for tomorrow?
C'est quoi la prévision pour demain ?
Sey kwah laa prey-vee-zyõn poor duh-mĩn ?

This is a heatwave.
C'est une canicule.
Sey_tun kaa-nee-kul.

Right now, it is overcast, but it should clear up by this evening.
Le ciel est couvert à l'instant, mais il devrait faire soleil d'ici le soir.
Luh syehl eh koo-vehr aa lĩn-stãn, meh eel duh-vreh fehr soh-ley-y dee-see luh swahr.

It is going to heat up in the afternoon.
Est-ce qu'il va faire plus chaud l'après-midi ?
Ehs-keel vah fehr plu shoh laa-preh mee-dee ?

What channel is the weather channel?
C'est quelle chaîne le canal météo ?
Sey kehl shehn luh kaa-naal mey-tey-oh ?

Tonight it will be below freezing.
Ce soir il va descendre en-dessous de zéro.
Suh swahr eel vah dey-sãndr ãn duh-soo duh zey-roh.

It's very windy outside.
Il y a beaucoup de vent dehors.
Eel ee yah boh-koo duh vãn duh-ohr.

It's going to be cold in the morning.
Il va faire très froid le matin.
Eeel vah fehr treh frwah luh maa-tĩn.

It's not raining, only drizzling.
Il ne pleut pas, il y a juste quelques gouttes qui tombent.
Eel nuh pluh pah, eel ee yah zhust kehl-kuh goot kee tõmb.

HOTEL

I would like to book a room.
J'aimerais réserver une chambre.
Zheh-muh-reh rey-zehr-vey un shãmbr.

I'd like a single room.
J'aimerais une chambre individuelle.
Zheh-muh-reh un shãmbr ĩn-dee-vee-du-ehl.

I'd like a suite.
J'aimerais avoir une suite.
Zheh-muh-reh aa-vwahr un sweet.

How much is the room per night?
Combien coûte la chambre par nuitée ?
Kõm-byĩn koot laa shãmbr paar nwee-tey ?

How much is the room with tax?
C'est quoi le prix de la chambre toutes taxes comprises ?
Sey kwah luh pree duh laa shãmbr toot taaks kõn-preez ?

When is the checkout time?
C'est quand l'heure de départ ?
Sey kãn luhr duh dey-pahr ?

I'd like a room with a nice view.
J'aimerais une chambre avec une belle vue.
Zheh-muh-reh un shãmbr aa-vehk un behl vu.

I'd like to order room service.
J'aimerais demander le service de chambre.
Zheh-muh-reh duh-mãn-dey luh sehr-vees duh shãmbr.

Let's go swim in the outdoor pool.
Allons nager dans la piscine extérieure.
Aa-lõn nah-zhey dãn laa pee-seen ehks-tey-ree-uhr.

Are pets allowed at the hotel?
Les animaux domestiques sont-ils permis dans l'hôtel ?
Ley_zaa-nee-moh doh-mehs-teek sõn_teel pehr-mee dãn loh-tehl ?

I would like a room on the first floor.
J'aimerais avoir une chambre au rez-de-chaussée.
Zheh-muh-reh aa-vwahr un shãmbr oh rey-duh-shoh-sey.

Can you send maintenance up to our room for a repair?
Pouvez-vous envoyer quelqu'un du service d'entretien à ma chambre
pour une réparation ?
*Poo-vey voo ãn-vwah-yey kehl-kũn du sehr-vees dãn-truh-tyĩn aa maa
shãmbr poor un rey-paa-raa-syõn ?*

I'm locked out of my room, could you unlock it?
Je suis embarré à l'extérieur de ma chambre, pouvez-vous le
dévérrouiller ?
*Zhuh swee_zãm-bah-rey aa lehks-tey-ree-uhr duh maa shãmbr, poo-vey
voo luh dey-vey-roo-yey ?*

Our door is jammed and won't open.
Notre porte est coincée et ne veut pas s'ouvrir.
Nohtr pohrt eh kwĩn-sey ey nuh vuh pah soo-vreer.

How do you work the shower?
Comment faire pour opérer la douche ?
Koh-mãn fehr poor oh-pey-rey laa doosh ?

Are the consumables in the room free?
Est-ce que les produits consommables dans la chambre sont gratuits ?
Ehs-kuh ley proh-dwee kõn-soh-maabl dãn laa shãmbr sõn graa-twee ?

What is my final bill for the stay, including incidentals?
C'est quoi mon addition finale pour le séjour, frais accessoires inclus ?
*Sey kwah mõn aa-dee-syõn fee-naal poor luh sey-zhoor, freh aak-seh-
swahr ĩn-klu ?*

Can you show me to my room?
Pouvez-vous me montrer ma chambre ?
Poo-vey voo muh mõn-trey maa shãmbr ?

Where can I get ice for my room?
Où pourrais-je trouver de la glace pour ma chambre ?
Oo poo-rehzh troo-vey duh laa glaas poor maa shãmbr ?

Do you have any rooms available?
Avez-vous des chambres disponibles ?
Aa-vey voo dey shãmbr dees-poh-neebl ?

Do you sell bottled water?
Vendez-vous de l'eau en bouteille ?
Vãn-dey voo duh loh ãn boo-teh-y ?

Our towels are dirty.
Nos serviettes sont à laver.
Noh sehr-vee-eht sõn_taa laa-vey.

Have you stayed at this hotel before?
Est-ce votre premier séjour chez cet hôtel ?
Ehs vohtr pruh-myey sey-zhoor shey seh_toh-tehl ?

How much is a room for two adults?
Combien coûte une chambre pour deux adultes ?
Kõm-byĩn koot un shãmbr poor duh_zaa-dult ?

Does the room come with a microwave?
Est-ce qu'il y a un micro-onde dans la chambre ?
Ehs-keel ee yah ũn mee-kroh-õnd dãn laa shãmbr ?

May I see the room first? That way I will know if I like it.
Puis-je voir la chambre en premier ? Comme ça je saurais si ça me plaît.
Pweezh vwahr laa shãmbr ãn pruh-myey ? Kohm sah zhuh soh-reh see saa muh pleh.

Do you have a room that is quieter?
Avez-vous une chambre moins bruyante ?
Aa-vey voo un shãmbr mwĩn bru-yãnt ?

How much is the deposit for my stay?
C'est combien l'acompte pour mon séjour ?
Sey kõm-byĩn laa-kõnt poor mõn sey-zhoor ?

Is the tap water drinkable at the hotel?
Est-ce que l'eau du robinet de l'hôtel est potable ?
Ehs-kuh loh du roh-bee-neh duh loh-tehl eh poh-taabl ?

Will there be any holds on my credit card?
Est-ce qu'il y aura une retenue de fonds sur ma carte de crédit ?
Ehs-keel ee oh-rah un ruh-tuh-nu duh fõn sur maa kaart duh krey-dee ?

Can I get a replacement room key?
Est-ce que je pourrais avoir une clé de rechange pour la chambre ?
Ehs-kuh zhuh poo-reh aa-vwahr un kley duh ruh-shãnzh poor laa shãmbr ?

How much is a replacement room key?
Combien coûte une clé de rechange pour la chambre ?
Kõm-byĩn koot un kley duh ruh-shãnzh poor laa shãmbr ?

Does the bathroom have a shower or a bathtub?
Est-ce qu'il y a une douche ou un bain dans la salle de bain ?
Ehs-keel ee yah un doosh oo ũn bĩn dãn laa saal duh bĩn ?

Are any of the channels on the TV available in English?
Est-ce qu'il y a des chaînes de télévision disponibles en anglais ?
Ehs-keel ee yah dey shehn duh tey-ley-vee-zyõn dees-poh-neebl ãn_nãn-gleh ?

I want a bigger room.
Je veux une chambre plus grande.
Zhuh vuh un shãmbr plu grãnd.

Do you serve breakfast in the morning?
Servez-vous un petit déjeuner le matin ?
Sehr-vey voo ũn puh-tee dey-zhuh-ney luh maa-tĩn ?

Oh, it's spacious.
Ah, c'est spacieux.
Ah, sey spaa-syuh.

My room is this way.
Ma chambre est par ici.
Maa shãmbr eh paar ee-see.

Straight down the hall.
Tout droit dans le corridor.
Too drwah dãn luh koh-ree-dohr.

Can you suggest a different hotel?
Pouvez-vous me suggérer un autre hôtel ?
Poo-vey voo muh sug-zhey-rey ũn_nohtr oh-tehl ?

Does the room have a safe for my valuables?
Est-ce qu'il y a un coffre dans la chambre pour mes objets de valeur ?
Ehs-keel ee yah ũn kohfr dãn laa shãmbr poor mey_zohb-zheh duh vaa-luhr ?

Please clean my room.
S'il vous plaît nettoyez ma chambre.
Seel voo pleh ney-twah-yey maa shãmbr.

Don't disturb me, please.
Ne me dérangez pas, s'il vous plaît.
Nuh muh dey-rãn-zhey pah, seel voo pleh.

Can you wake me up at noon?
Pouvez-vous me réveiller à midi ?
Poo-vey voo muh rey-vey-ey aa mee-dee ?

I would like to check out of my hotel room.
J'aimerais régler la note pour ma chambre.
Zheh-muh-reh rey-gley laa noht poor maa shãmbr.

Please increase the cleanup duty of my hotel room.
S'il vous plaît augmentez la fréquence du nettoyage de ma chambre.
Seel voo pleh ohg-mãn-tey laa frey-kãns du neh-twah-yaazh duh maa shãmbr.

Is the Marriott any good?
Le Marriott est-il bon ?
Luh maa-ree-oht eh-teel bõn ?

Is it expensive to stay at the Marriott?
Est-ce que ça coûte cher de rester au Marriott ?
Ehs-kuh saa koot shehr duh rehs-tey oh maa-ree-oht ?

I think our room has bedbugs.
Je crois qu'il y a des punaises de lit dans notre chambre.
Zhuh krwah keel ee yah dey pu-nehz duh lee dãn nohtr shãmbr.

Can you send an exterminator to our room?
Pouvez-vous envoyer un exterminateur à notre chambre ?
Poo-vey voo ãn-vwah-yey ũn_nehks-tehr-mee-naa-tuhr aa nohtr shãmbr ?

I need to speak to your manager.
J'ai besoin de parler avec votre superviseur.
Zhey buh-zwĩn duh paar-ley aa-vehk vohtr su-pehr-vee-zuhr.

Do you have the number to corporate?
Avez-vous le numéro du siège social ?
Aa-vey voo luh nu-mey-roh du see-ehzh soh-see-aal ?

Does the hotel shuttle go to the casino?
Est-ce que la navette de l'hôtel se déplace au casino ?
Ehs-kuh laa naa-veht duh loh-tehl suh dey-plaas oh kaa-zee-noh ?

Can you call me when the hotel shuttle is on its way?
Pouvez-vous m'appeler lorsque la navette de l'hôtel est en route ?
Poo-vey voo maa-puh-ley lohr-skuh laa naa-veht duh loh-tehl eh_tãn root ?

Can we reserve this space for a party?
Pouvons-nous réserver cette espace pour une fête ?
Poo-võn noo rey-zehr-vey seht ehs-pahs poor un feht ?

What is the guest limit for reserving an area?
Quelle est la limite d'invités pour réserver une espace ?
Kehl eh laa lee-meet dĩn-vee-tey poor rey-zehr-vey un ehs-pahs ?

What are the rules for reserving an area?
Quelles sont les règles pour réserver une espace ?
Kehl sõn ley rehgl poor rey-zehr-vey un ehs-pahs ?

Can we serve or drink alcohol during our get together?
Pouvons-nous servir ou boire de l'alcool pendant notre réunion ?
Poo-võn noo sehr-veer oo bwahr duh laal-kohl pãn-dãn nohtr rey-u-nyõn ?

I would like to complain about a noisy room next to us.
J'aimerais déposer une plainte au sujet de la chambre bruyante à côté de la nôtre.
Zheh-muh-reh dey-poh-zey un plĩnt oh su-zhey duh laa shãmbr bru-yãnt aa koh-tey duh laa nohtr.

We have some personal items missing from our room.
Il y a quelques articles personnels qui manquent de notre chambre.
Eel ee yah kehl-kuh_zaar-teekl pehr-soh-nehl kee mãnk duh nohtr shãmbr.

SPORTS AND EXERCISE

Can we walk faster?
Pouvons-nous marcher plus rapidement ?
Poo-võn noo maar-shey plu raa-peed-mãn ?

Do you want to go to a drag race track?
Voulez-vous aller à une piste de course de vitesse ?
Voo-ley voo aa-ley aa un peest duh koors duh vee-tehs ?

Are you taking a walk?
Vous allez vous promener ?
Voo_zaa-ley voo proh-muh-ney ?

Do you want to jog for a kilometer or two?
Voulez-vous faire quelques kilomètres de jogging ?
Voo-ley voo fehr kehl-kuh kee-loh-mehtr duh djoh-geeng ?

How about fast walking?
Et la marche rapide ?
Ey laa maarsh raa-peed ?

Would you like to walk with me?
Voulez-vous marcher avec moi ?
Voo-ley voo maar-shey aa-vehk mwah ?

He is a really good player.
Il est un très bon joueur.
Eel eh_tũn treh bõn zhoo-uhr.

I feel bad that they traded him to the other team.
Je suis déçu qu'ils l'ont échangé contre un joueur de l'autre équipe.
Zhuh swee dey-su keel lõn ey-shãn-zhey kõntr ũn zhoo-uhr duh lohtr ey-keep.

Did you see that home run?

Vous avez vu ce coup de circuit ?

Voo_zaa-vey vu suh koo duh seer-kwee ?

I have been a fan of that team for many years.

Je suis fan de cette équipe depuis plusieurs années.

Zhuh swee faan duh seht ey-keep duh-pwee plu-zyuhr_zaa-ney.

Who is your favorite team?

C'est qui votre équipe préférée ?

Sey kee vohtr ey-keep prey-fey-rey ?

Pelé is my favorite player.

Pelé c'est mon joueur préféré.

Pey-ley sey mõn zhoo-uhr prey-fey-rey.

Do you like soccer?

Vous aimez le football ?

Voo_zeh-mey luh foot-bahl ?

Do you watch American football?

Suivez-vous le football américain ?

Swee-vey voo luh foot-bahl aa-mey-ree-kĩn ?

Are there any games on right now?

Y-a-t-il des matchs qui tournent à l'instant ?

Ee-yah teel dey maatch kee toorn aa lĩn-stãn ?

That was a bad call by the ref.

C'était une mauvaise décision de la part de l'arbitre.

Sey-tey un moh-vehz dey-see-zyõn duh laa pahr duh laar-beetr.

I put a lot of money on this game.

J'ai parié beaucoup d'argent sur ce match.

Zhey paa-ree-ey boh-koo daar-zhãn sur suh maatch.

His stats have been incredible this season.

Ses statistiques sont incroyables cette saison.

Sey staa-tees-teek sõn ĩn-krwah-yaabl seht seh-zõn.

Do you want to play baseball today?
Voulez-vous jouer au baseball aujourd'hui ?
Voo-ley voo zhoo-ey oh beyz-bahl oh-zhoor-dwee ?

Let's go to the soccer field and practice.
Allons au terrain de foot pour pratiquer.
Aa-lõn oh tey-rĩn duh foot poor praa-tee-key.

I am barely working up a sweat.
À peine je transpire.
Aa pehn zhuh trãns-peer.

Let's go to the gym and lift weights.
Allons à la salle de sport faire de la musculation.
Aa-lõn aa laa saal duh spohr fehr duh laa mus-ku-laa-syõn.

Give me more weights.
Ajoutez-moi des haltères.
Aa-zhoo-tey mwah dey_zaal-tehr.

Take some weights off.
Enlevez quelques haltères.
Ãn-luh-vey kehl-kuh_zaal-tehr.

Will you spot me?
Pouvez-vous m'assurer ?
Poo-vey voo maa-su-rey ?

How long do you want to run on the treadmill?
Combien de temps vous voulez courir sur le tapis roulant ?
Kõm-byĩn duh tãn voo voo-ley koo-reer sur luh taa-pee roo-lãn ?

Is this the best gym in the area?
Est-ce la meilleure salle de sport dans ce quartier ?
Ehs laa meh-yuhr saal duh spohr dãn suh kaar-tyey ?

Do I need a membership to enter this gym?
Est-ce que j'ai besoin d'un abonnement pour utiliser cette salle de sport ?
Ehs-kuh zhey buh-zwĩn dũn_naa-bohn-mãn poor u-tee-lee-zey seht saal duh spohr ?

Do you have trial memberships for tourists?
Avez-vous un abonnement provisoire pour les touristes ?
Aa-vey voo ũn_naa-bohn-mãn proh-vee-zwahr poor ley too-reest ?

My muscles are still sore from the last workout.
Mes muscles me font encore mal depuis la dernière séance
d'entraînement.
*Mey muskl muh fõn ãn-kahr maal duh-pwee laa dehr-nyehr sey-ãns dãn-
treh-nuh-mãn.*

Give me a second while I adjust this.
Donnez-moi un moment pendant que je régle ça.
Doh-ney mwah ũn moh-mãn pãn-dãn kuh zhuh rehgl sah.

Time to hit the steam room!
C'est l'heure du hammam !
Sey luhr du aa-maam !
You can put that in my locker.
Vous pouvez mettre ça dans mon casier.
Voo poo-vey mehtr sah dãn mõn kah-zyey.

I think we have to take turns on this machine.
Je crois qu'on doit aller à tour de rôle sur cette machine.
Zhuh krwah kõn dwah aa-ley aa toor duh rohl sur seht maa-sheen.

Make sure to wipe down the equipment when you are done.
N'oubliez pas d'essuyer l'équipement lorsque vous en finissez avec.
*Noo-blee-ey pah dehs-wee-ey ley-keep-mãn lohr-skuh voo_zãn fee-nee-
sey aa-vehk.*

Is there a time limit on working out here?
Y-a-t-il un délai pour s'entraîner ici ?
Ee-yah teel ũn dey-leh poor sãn-trey-ney ee-see ?

We should enter a marathon.
On devrait s'inscrire pour un marathon.
Õn duh-vreh sĩn-skreer poor ũn maa-raa-tõn.

How has your diet been going?
Comment va ton régime ?
Koh-mãn vah tõn rey-zheem ?

Are you doing keto?
Vous faites le régime cétogène ?
Voo feht luh rey-zheem sey-toh-zhehn ?

Make sure to stay hydrated while you work out.
N'oubliez pas de rester hydraté lorsque vous vous entraînez.
Noo-blee-ey pah duh rehs-tey ee-draa-tey lohr-skuh voo voo_zãn-trey-ney.

I'll go grab you a protein shake.
Je vais aller vous chercher un shake protéiné.
Zhuh veh aa-ley voo shehr-shey ũn sheyk proh-tey-ee-ney.

Do you want anything else? I'm buying.
Vous voulez autre chose ? C'est moi qui achète.
Voo voo-ley ohtr shohz ? Sey mwah kee aa-sheht.

I need to buy some equipment before I play that.
Je dois acheter certains équipements avant de jouer à ça.
Zhuh dwah aa-shuh-tey sehr-tĩn_zey-keep-mãn aa-vãn duh zhoo-ey aa sah.

Do you want to spar?
Tu veux faire du sparring ?
Tu vuh fehr du spah-reeng ?

Full contact sparring.
Sparring plein-contact.
Spah-reeng plĩn kõn-taakt.

Just a simple practice round.
Juste une petite ronde d'entraînement.
Just un puh-teet rõnd dãn-trehn-mãn.

Do you want to wrestle?
Tu veux faire du catch ?
Tu vuh fehr du kaatch ?

What are the rules to play this game?
Quels sont les règles du jeu ?
Kehl sõn ley rehgl du zhuh ?

Do we need a referee?
Est-ce qu'on a besoin d'un arbitre ?
Ehs-kõn_nah buh-zwĩn dũn_naar-beetr ?

I don't agree with that call.
Je suis pas d'accord avec cette décision.
Zhuh swee pah daa-kohr aa-vehk seht dey-see-zyõn.

Can we get another opinion on that score?
On peut avoir un autre avis sur ce score ?
Õn puh aa-vwahr ũn_nohtr aa-vee sur suh skohr ?

How about a game of table tennis?
Qu'en diriez-vous d'un match de tennis de table ?
Kãn dee-ree-ey voo dũn maatch duh teh-nees duh taabl ?

Do you want to team up?
Voulez-vous faire équipe ?
Voo-ley voo fehr ey-keep ?

Goal!
Goal !
Gohl !

Homerun!
Coup de circuit !
Koo duh seer-kwee !

Touchdown!
Touche !
Toosh !

Score!
Score !
Skohr !

On your mark, get set, go!
À vos marques, prêts, partez !
Aa voh maark, preh, paar-tey !

Do you want to borrow my equipment?
Vous voulez emprunter mon équipement ?
Voo voo-ley ãm-prũn-tey mõn_ney-keep-mãn ?

Hold the game for a second.
Arrêtez le match pour un instant.
Aa-reh-tey luh maatch poor ũn_nĩn-stãn.

I don't understand the rules of this game.
Je comprends pas les règles de ce jeu.
Zhuh kõm-prãn pah ley rehgl duh suh zhuh.

Timeout!
Arrêt !
Aa-reh !

Can we switch sides?
On peut échanger de cõtés ?
Õn puh ey-shãn-zhey duh koh-tey ?

There is something wrong with my equipment.
Il y a un problème avec mon équipement.
Eel ee yah ũn proh-blehm aa-vehk mõn_ney-keep-mãn.

How about another game?
On joue un autre ?
Õn zhoo ũn_nohtr ?

I would like a do over of that last game.
J'aimerais refaire cette dernière partie.
Zheh-muh-reh ruh-fehr seht dehr-nyehr paar-tee.

Do want to go golfing?
Vous voulez aller faire du golf ?
Voo voo-ley aa-ley fehr du gohlf ?

Where can we get a golf cart?
Où pouvons-nous obtenir un chariot de golf ?
Oo poo-võn noo ohb-tuh-neer ũn shaa-ree-oh duh gohlf ?

Do you have your own clubs?
Avez-vous vos propres clubs de golf ?
Aa-vey voo voh proh-pruh klub duh gohlf ?

Would you like to play with my spare clubs?
Aimeriez-vous jouer avec mes doubles de clubs ?
Eh-muh-ree-ey voo zhoo-ey aa-vehk mey doobl duh klub ?

How many holes do you want to play?
Combien de trous vous voulez jouer ?
Kõm-byĩn duh troo voo voo-ley zhoo-ey ?

Do I have to be a member of this club to play?
Est-ce que je dois être membre de ce club pour jouer ?
Ehs-kuh zhuh dwah ehtr mãmbr duh suh klub poor zhoo-ey ?

Let me ice this down, it is sore.
Laissez-moi mettre de la glace dessus, il fait mal.
Leh-sey mwah mehtr duh laa glaas duh-su, eel feh maal.

I can't keep up with you, slow down.
Je peux pas vous suivre, ralentissez.
Zhuh puh pah voo sweevr, raa-lãn-tee-sey.

Let's pick up the pace a little bit.
Accélérons un peu le rhythme.
Aak-sey-ley-rõn ũn puh luh reetm.

Do you need me to help you with that?
Vous avez besoin d'aide avec ça ?
Voo_zaa-vey buh-zwĩn dehd aa-vehk sah ?

Am I being unfair?
C'est injuste de ma part ?
Sey ĩn-zhust duh maa pahr ?

Let's switch teams for the next game.
Échangeons d'équipe pour la prochaine partie.
Ey-shãn-zhõn dey-keep poor laa proh-shehn paar-tee.

Hand me those weights.
Passez-moi ces haltères.
Pah-sey mwah sey_zaal-tehr.

THE FIRST 24 HOURS AFTER ARRIVING

When did you arrive?
Quand est-ce que vous êtes arrivé ?
Kãn_tehs-kuh voo_zeht aa-ree-vey ?

That was a very pleasant flight.
C'était un vol très agréable.
Sey-tey ũn vohl treh_zaag-rey-aabl.

Yes, it was a very peaceful trip. Nothing bad happened.
Oui, c'était un voyage très paisible. Rien de négatif s'est passé.
Wee, sey-tey ũn vwah-yaazh treh peh-zeebl. Ree-ĩn duh ney-gaa-teef sey pah-sey.

I have jetlag so need to lay down for a bit.
Je suis fatigué avec le décalage horaire, je dois me reposer un peu.
Zhuh swee faa-tee-gey aa-vehk luh dey-kaa-laazh oh-rehr, zhuh dwah muh ruh-poh-zey ũn puh.

No, that was my first time flying.
Non, c'était mon premier vol.
Nõn, sey-tey mõn pruh-myey vohl.

When is the check-in time?
C'est à quelle heure l'enregistrement ?
Sey_taa kehl uhr lãn-ruh-zhee-struh-mãn ?

Do we need to get cash?
On a besoin d'obtenir des espèces ?
Õn ah buh-zwĩn dohb-tuh-neer dey_zehs-pehs ?

How much money do you have on you?
Combien d'argent vous avez sur vous ?
Kõm-byĩn daar-zhãn voo_zaa-vey sur voo ?

How long do you want to stay here?
Combien de temps vous voulez rester ici ?
Kõm-byĩn duh tãn voo voo-ley rehs-tey ee-see ?

Do we have all of our luggage?
Est-ce qu'on a tous nos bagages ?
Ehs-kõn_nah too noh baa-gaazh ?

Let's walk around the city a bit before checking in.
Allons se promener un peu dans la ville avant l'enregistrement.
Aa-lõn suh proh-muh-ney ũn puh dãn laa veel aa-vãn lãn-ruh-zhee-struh-mãn.

When is check-in time for our hotel?
C'est à quelle heure l'enregistrement pour notre hôtel ?
Sey_taa kehl uhr lãn-ruh-zhee-struh-mãn poor nohtr oh-tehl ?

I'll call the landlord and let him know we landed.
Je vais appeler le propriétaire et lui informer qu'on a attérit.
Zhuh veh aa-puh-ley luh proh-pree-ey-tehr ey lwee ĩn-fohr-mey kôn_nah aa-tey-ree.

Let's find a place to rent a car.
Trouvons un lieu pour louer une voiture.
Troo-vôn ũn lyuh poor loo-ey un vwah-tur.

Let's walk around the hotel room and make sure it's correct.
Faisons le tour de la chambre d'hôtel pour s'assurer qu'il est bien.
Feh-zõn luh toor duh laa shãmbr doh-tehl poor saa-su-rey keel eh byĩn.

We'll look at our apartment and make sure everything is in order.
On va jeter un coup d'œil sur notre appartement pour s'assurer que tout est en ordre.
Õn vah zhuh-tey ũn koo duh-y sur nohtr aa-paar-tuh-mãn poor saa-su-rey kuh too_teh_tãn_nohr-dr.

THE LAST 24 HOURS BEFORE LEAVING

Where are the passports?
Où sont les passeports ?
Oo sõn ley paas-pohr ?

Did you fill out the customs forms?
Avez-vous rempli le formulaire des douanes ?
Aa-vey voo rãm-plee luh fohr-mu-lehr dey doo-aan ?

Make sure to pack everything.
Assurez-vous d'avoir tout mis dans les bagages.
Aa-su-rey voo daa-vwahr too mee dãn ley baa-gaazh.

Where are we going?
On va où ?
Õn vah oo ?

Which flight are we taking?
On prend quel vol ?
Õn prãn kehl vohl ?

Check your pockets.
Vérifiez vos poches.
Vey-ree-fee-ey voh pohsh.

I need to declare some things for customs.
J'ai des trucs à déclarer aux douanes.
Zhey dey truk aa dey-klaa-rey oh doo-aan.

No, I have nothing to declare.
Non, je n'ai rien à déclarer.
Nôn, zhuh ney ryĩn_naa dey-klaa-rey.

What is the checkout time?
C'est à quelle heure le départ de l'hôtel ?
Sey_taa kehl uhr luh dey-pahr duh loh-tehl ?

Make sure your phone is charged.
Assurez-vous que votre téléphone est chargé.
Aa-su-rey voo kuh vohtr tey-ley-fon eh shaar-zhey.

Is there a fee attached to this?
Y-a-t-il un frais pour cela ?
Ee-yah teel ũn freh poor suh-lah ?

Do we have any outstanding bills to pay?
Est-ce qu'il nous reste des frais à payer ?
Eh-skeel noo rehst dey freh aa pey-ey ?

What time does our flight leave?
À quelle heure notre vol décolle ?
Aa kehl uhr nohtr vohl dey-kohl ?

What time do we need to be in the airport?
À quelle heure on doit être à l'aéroport ?
Aa kehl uhr õn dwah ehtr aa laa-ey-roh-pohr ?

How bad is the traffic going in the direction of the airport?
Combien il y a d'encombrement en direction de l'aéroport ?
Kõm-byĩn eel ee yah dãn-kõm-bruh-mãn ãn dee-rehk-syõn duh laa-ey-roh-pohr ?

Are there any detours we can take?
Y-a-t-il des détours qu'on peut prendre ?
Ee-yah teel dey dey-toor kõn puh prãndr ?

What haven't we seen from our list since we've been down here?
Qu'est-ce qu'il nous reste sur notre liste qu'on n'a pas vu depuis qu'on est ici ?
Kehs-keel noo rehst sur nohtr leest kõn_nah pah vu duh-pwee kõn_neh_tee-see ?

We should really buy some souvenirs here.
On devrait vraiment acheter quelques souvenirs ici.
Õn duh-vreh vreh-mãn aa-shuh-tey kehl-kuh soo-vuh-neer ee-see.

Do you know any shortcuts that will get us there faster?

Connaissez-vous des raccourcis qui nous feront arriver plus rapidement ?

Koh-neh-sey voo dey raa-koor-see kee noo fuh-rõn aa-ree-vey plus raa-peed-mãn ?

GPS the location and save it.

Cherchez le lieu sur le GPS et enregistrez-le.

Shehr-shey luh lyuh sur luh zhey-pey-ehs ey ãn-ruh-zhee-strey luh.

Are the items we're bringing back allowed on the plane?

Est-ce que les articles qu'on rammène sont permis sur l'avion ?

Ehs-kuh ley_zaar-teekl kõn raa-mehn sõn pehr-mee sur laa-vee-õn ?

We should call our family back home before leaving.

On devrait appeler notre famille à la maison avant de partir.

Õn duh-vreh aa-puh-ley nohtr faa-mee-y aa laa meh-zõn aa-vãn duh paar-teer.

Make sure the pet cage is locked.

Assurez-vous que la cage d'animal est fermée.

Aa-su-rey voo kuh laa kaazh daa-nee-maal eh fehr-mey.

Go through your luggage again.

Revoyez vos bagages encore une fois.

Ruh-vwah-yey voh baa-gaazh ãn-kahr un fwah.

MORE FROM LINGO MASTERY

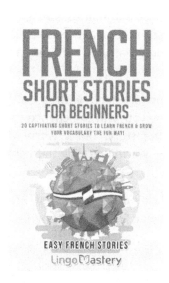

Do you know what the hardest thing for a French learner is?

Finding PROPER reading material that they can handle...which is precisely the reason we've written this book!

Teachers love giving out tough, expert-level literature to their students, books that present many new problems to the reader and force them to search for words in a dictionary every five minutes — it's not entertaining, useful or motivating for the student at all, and many soon give up on learning at all!

In this book we have compiled 20 easy-to-read, compelling and fun stories that will allow you to expand your vocabulary and give you the tools to improve your grasp of the wonderful French tongue.

How French Short Stories for Beginners works:

- Each story will involve an important lesson of the tools in the French language (Verbs, Adjectives, Past Tense, Giving Directions, and more), involving an interesting and entertaining story with realistic dialogues and day-to-day situations.

- The summaries follow a synopsis in French and in English of what you just read, both to review the lesson and for you to see if you understood what the tale was about.

- At the end of those summaries, you'll be provided with a list of the most relevant vocabulary involved in the lesson, as well as slang and sayings that you may not have understood at first glance!

- Finally, you'll be provided with a set of tricky questions in French, providing you with the chance to prove that you learned something in the story. Don't worry if you don't know the answer to any — we will provide them immediately after, but no cheating!

So look no further! Pick up your copy of **French Short Stories for Beginners** and start learning French right now!

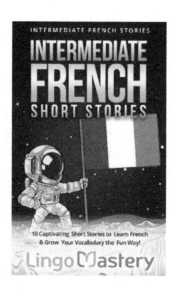

Improve your French skills and grow your vocabulary with these 10 entertaining French short stories!

The best part of learning a new language is experiencing the culture and diving into activities that will enrich your life and vocabulary. The best way to learn a new language is by reading, and in this French book you will find yourself turning page after page to get to the end of each captivating story that will engage your mind and help you improve your French.

In this book you will find:

10 captivating short stories that develop in circumstances such as traveling, personal relationships, among other topics that you will find easy to relate to.

The stories are broken down into manageable chapters, so you always make progress with the story.

Carefully written stories with you as an **intermediate level reader in mind**, using straightforward grammar and commonly used words so you can enjoy reading while learning new grammatical structures without being overwhelmed.

Plenty of natural dialogues in each story that you would actually use in an everyday conversation, which will drastically improve your speaking and comprehension ability at the same time!

At the end of each chapter there will be a comprehensive guide specially designed for intermediate level readers, it will take you through a summary of each story followed by a vocabulary of some of the words from the story to make sure that you understand the story fully.

Chapter by chapter you will find yourself effortlessly reading each story. Not struggling like in basic textbooks or boring reads. You will get involved by reading the dialogue of the characters by learning how to express yourself in different contexts and more importantly by learning new French words that will get you closer to your goal of becoming fully conversational!

Is conversational French turning a little too tricky for you? Do you have no idea on how to order a meal or book a room at a hotel?

If your answer to any of the previous questions was 'Yes', then this book is for you!

If there's even been something tougher than learning the grammar rules of a new language, it's finding the way to speak with other people in that tongue. Any student knows this – we can try our best at practicing, but you always want to avoid making embarrassing mistakes or not getting your message through correctly.

'How do I get out of this situation?' many students ask themselves, to no avail, but no answer is forthcoming.

Until now.

We have compiled **MORE THAN ONE HUNDRED French Stories for Beginners** along with their translations, allowing new French speakers to have the necessary tools to begin studying how to set a meeting, rent a car or tell a doctor that they don't feel well! We're not wasting time here with conversations that don't go anywhere: if you want to know how to solve problems (while learning a ton of French along the way, obviously), this book is for you!

How Conversational French Dialogues works:

- Each new chapter will have a fresh, new story between two people who wish to solve a common, day-to-day issue that you will surely encounter in real life.

- A French version of the conversation will take place first, followed by an English translation. This ensures that you fully understood just what it was that they were saying!

- Before and after the main section of the book, we shall provide you with an introduction and conclusion that will offer you important strategies, tips and tricks to allow you to get the absolute most out of this learning material.

- That's about it! Simple, useful and incredibly helpful; you will NOT need another conversational French book once you have begun reading and studying this one!

We want you to feel comfortable while learning the tongue; after all, no language should be a barrier for you to travel around the world and expand your social circles!

So look no further! Pick up your copy of **Conversational French Dialogues** and start learning French right now!

CONCLUSION

Congratulations! You have reached the end of this book and learned over **1,500** ways to express yourself in the French language! It is a moment to celebrate, since you are now much closer to achieving complete fluency of the French tongue.

However, the learning simply cannot end here – you may have unlocked a massive amount of incredibly useful day-to-day phrases that will get you anywhere you need to go, but are you prepared to use them correctly? Furthermore, will you actually remember them during your travels when faced with one of the situations we've presented in this book?

Only by continuously studying the material found in these chapters will you ever be able to summon the words and phrases encountered above, since it isn't a matter of *what* the phrases are but *how* and *when* to use them. Knowing the exact context is crucial, as well as reinforcing your knowledge with other materials.

For this reason, we have created a quick list of tips to make the most of this French Phrasebook and expanding your vocabulary and grasp of the French language:

1. **Practice every day:** You can be very good at something thanks to the gift of natural talent, but practice is the only way to *stay* good. Make sure to constantly pick up the book and read the words, saying them out loud and taking note of your mistakes so you can correct them.

2. **Read while listening:** A very popular and modern way of learning a new language is by using the RwL (reading while listening) method. It has been proven that this method can greatly boost fluency, help you ace language tests, and improve your learning in other subjects. Feel free to try out our audiobooks and other listening materials in French – you'll love them!

3. **Studying in groups:** It's always best to go on an adventure together – even if it's a language adventure! You'll enjoy yourself more if you can find someone who wants to learn with you. Look to friends, your partner, your family members, or colleagues for support, and maybe they can even help you make the process easier and quicker!

4. **Creating your own exercises:** This book provides you with plenty of material for your learning processes, and you will probably be happy with reading it every time you can...however, you need to increase the difficulty by looking for other words and phrases in the French language which you don't know the pronunciation to and trying to decipher them for yourself. Use the knowledge you've gained with previous lessons to discover entirely new words!

With that said, we have now fully concluded this French Phrasebook, which will surely accelerate your learning to new levels. Don't forget to follow every tip we've included and keep an eye out for our additional French materials.